Exploring **World** Mission

C O N T E X T & C H A L L E N G E S

B R Y A N T L. M Y E R S

Exploring World Mission

Bryant L. Myers

Printed in the United States of America.

Published by World Vision International
800 West Chestnut Avenue
Monrovia, California 91016-3198 USA

Editor in Chief: Edna Valdez. Senior Editor: Rebecca Russell. Copyediting: Bob Newman. Creative Direction and Production: Jim McAllister and Marti Chavarria. Page design and type-setting: Richard Sears. Cover design: Judy Walker.

ISBN 1-887983-51-1

The graphic pages of this book are also available in CD-ROM as Power Point® slides. Contact World Vision Resources for more information at www.vorldvisionresources.com.

♲ Printed on acid-free recycled paper.

Other titles by
Bryant L. Myers

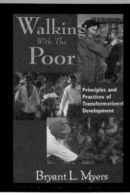 

Contents

The Church in the World

Challenges to Mission

Foreword

Suppose a brother or sister is without clothes and daily food. If one of you says to him, "Go, I wish you well; keep warm and well fed," but does nothing about his physical needs, what good is it? In the same way, faith by itself, if it is not accompanied by action, is dead (James 2:15-17, NIV).

This is an extraordinary time to be a follower of Christ. The church's work in the world has perhaps never been more critical than it is today, and this book combines fresh facts, maps and conclusions to demonstrate why we as Christians must act now.

Today the body of Christ stands at a crossroads. The world is changing at an unprecedented rate, the gap between rich and poor continues to widen, and the need to hear the Good News of the gospel remains as urgent as it was thousands of years ago. At the same time, we have unparalleled opportunities to come alongside people in need of spiritual and physical care, serving as Jesus did among people in need.

As we stand at this crossroads, *Exploring World Mission* provides a road map that details the world's spiritual, political, social and economic landscapes. In these pages, you will explore the transformation of the church's mission, the current condition of the world and the church, and contemporary challenges to Christian mission.

If you are like me, your first reaction to the world's needs may be that these issues seem so much larger than you are. Yet as Christians, we not only have the opportunity but also the responsibility to ask ourselves how we will respond to these very real needs. Why should we bother? Because the statistics on the following pages represent real people like you and me, each one a person for whom God intends fullness of life. As Christians, we are uniquely equipped to share that fullness as we point the way not only to physical wholeness but to spiritual hope as well.

Jesus' parable of the Good Samaritan is a familiar story that answers the fundamental question, "Who is my neighbor?" Challenged by a Jewish scholar of scripture, Jesus responded with this poignant story that casts a Samaritan—a social outcast among Jews—as a hero when he cared for the stranger left half dead on the roadside. In contrast, Jewish religious leaders who were passing by ignored the needs of the man, choosing instead to walk on the other side of the road. Jesus' message was this: The Jewish leaders had the right beliefs, but they didn't transfer their beliefs into action. The Samaritan not only had the right beliefs, he acted on those beliefs.

Today our churches are filled with people with the right beliefs. Yet God calls us to act on what we believe. Will we care for a "half dead" world crying for help or choose to walk on the other side of the road?

Separate, we are just individuals, but together we can multiply the gospel's impact on the world. May you be blessed as you grasp new opportunities to serve God and your neighbor.

Rich Stearns
President, World Vision United States

Introduction

This is a book about God's call for us to embrace and love a good and tragic world. Images, glimpses and patterns are presented in an effort to stretch us beyond the world as secular media and cynics too often present it.

This book attempts to portray the world in a wide variety of ways, looking at it through many different lenses. Some of the patterns simply describe what is. Others show how the world is changing. Still other patterns try to provide a correction for common perceptions of the world. The hope is that we can see the world a little more as God sees it: As a treasure worthy of the death of God's Son.

The purpose of this book is to help broaden and challenge our thinking about Christian mission. God's world is more than a collection of saved believers and lost souls. There is much that God loves in this world and that reflects God's will. There is much that God hates.

We need to learn to think holistically, comprehensively and inclusively. While mission strategy necessarily focuses our efforts, mission research must do the opposite. We need to embrace the complexity, diversity and inconsistency of God's world. By opening up our minds and perceptions, the Holy Spirit gains an opportunity to show us new things and to call for improvement in old ways.

The evangelical mission movement of the last century was brilliantly focused on evangelism, but was not so good at seeing and responding to the racism, genocide and marginalization that were characteristic of that era. Christian mission was trapped in a worldview that focused almost solely on the spiritual and the saving of souls, both very good and necessary concerns of Christian mission. But we missed the emergence of evil on a colossal scale. In addition to two world wars and a cold war that killed tens of millions, eight genocides took place in the 20th century. Were it not for a few brave prophets from the developing world at Lausanne 1974, these issues might not have made it onto the mission agenda at all.

But this book is more than numbers and maps. I also hope that the reader will find this a manual for prayer. This book describes the world that Jesus died for. Even as you see the sad things that make up today's world, remember that Jesus' response to disheartening events, such as the impending fall of Jerusalem, was tears.

The world you are about to see is God's. Every good and tragic person and situation in today's world belongs to God and is the object of his loving concern. As you read this book, please pray. Take some time in silence from time to time. Listen for the quiet word of the Spirit of God. Somewhere in these pages there may be a word for you from God.

The good news

There is good news in God's world, although we don't hear much news about this from the media and the "experts." Child mortality is down over 100% since 1960. Life expectancy is on the rise everywhere except in parts of Africa, where AIDS is reversing these increases. Fertility rates have declined in all regions since 1945, except in Africa.

There has been an increase in human development, measured by income, education and life expectancy, in all the world's regions since 1960. There have been sharp increases in primary school attendance and in adult literacy, especially among women. Access to safe water has increased from 36% of the world's children in 1965 to 77% today. Christian mission is now global and universal. Missionaries come from everywhere and go to everywhere. The liberalism of the church in the North is being corrected by the biblical faithfulness of the church in the South. More people are praying strategically than at any other time in human history.

At the same time, God's world is in a period of rapid change. Communications and information technology are creat-

ing rapid and deep-seated shifts in many areas of life. Internet usage is increasing at a rate twenty times faster than radio and television did in their day. Science is making discovery after discovery. Country after country is moving away from the rule of the big man or the military toward embryonic democracies.

The not so good news

The first decade of the 21st century reflects the chaotic aftermath of the breakdown of a world order that had been in place since the end of World War II. Sadly, early expectations that the post-cold war period would see reduced levels of conflict and broader economic prosperity have been disappointed. Warlords exploit ethnicity and religion for power and personal economic gain in private little wars, while the international community struggles to find a framework for global leadership and peace building.

There are wars and rumors of wars. Parts of the world are suffering in chaotic vacuums as conflicts, failed governments and non-existent economies make peace and rule of law impossible. Other parts of the world are struggling to recover from the economic excesses of the 1990s and are struggling with materialism. Everywhere terrorism, criminalized states and fundamentalism are creating fear and uncertainty.

The poverty in which so many of the world's children live remains intractable and growing. While the percentage of people living in extreme poverty—

defined as less than US$1 a day—has fallen somewhat from 1987 to 1998, the number of people living on less than US$1 a day remains unacceptably high at 1.2 billion. Every day, diseases largely preventable in the West kill 30,500 children under the age of five in the less developed areas of the world. Everyone agrees that children are our future, and yet, since children are not a political constituency, children still too often remain invisible to governments and many others.

Deep ironies and fundamental changes are multiplying. The fastest-growing group of malnourished people are those 1.2 billion who are eating too much of the wrong kind of food, a number that almost matches the number of underfed and malnourished in the developing world. The three richest people in the world have assets exceeding the combined gross domestic product of the 48 least-developed countries. Too many countries pay more to debt service than they do for public services.

The Christian church

The center of gravity of the Christian church has moved to the South, where more than 50% of today's Christians and 70% of today's evangelicals live. Latin America is the largest continent of Christians, with dramatic shifts taking place between historic Roman Catholic dominance and free-wheeling Pentecostalism. Africa has the fastest-growing church. The churches of Asia are experiencing significant growth and, although

still a minority religion, are becoming centers of missionary sending and compassionate giving.

This good news of church growth has been accompanied by some profound contradictions. The growth of the church in Africa, Asia and Latin America, and the continuing strength of the church in the United States, has not been accompanied by widespread changes in social, economic and political behavior reflecting the values of the kingdom of God. On the contrary, we see more poverty, injustice, immoral and unethical behavior, materialism and violence. Everywhere, and for every church, the critical question is what kind of Christians are we making?

The poor and the lost are often invisible to the Christian church. Within a band reaching across North Africa, including most of the Sahel, through the Middle East, and into central Asia, the northern part of the Indian subcontinent, Southeast Asia and western China, live 1.6 billion people who have little chance to hear the good news of Jesus Christ unless someone goes to tell them. Eighty-five percent of the world's poorest countries are located in this same part of the world.

Driving Forces

"Driving forces" is a phrase intended to name the major forces shaping human history. Driving forces cannot be controlled or ignored, but they can be used. An effective mission strategy or organization recognizes these forces and positions itself so that the driving forces push the organization toward its mission and future well-being.

The Holy Spirit of God

As Christians, we know that human history is going somewhere and that it has a purpose. The most fundamental driving force at work in the world is the Holy Spirit. As Christians, we believe in a king who has come and whose kingdom is both established and is yet coming. As Christians, we are part of this kingdom and our mission is derived from our desire to be obedient to this call in our lives. No driving force or global trend can ultimately divert God from what God has chosen to do.

Yet God does not work alone in human history. There is clear evidence of an Evil One, who is also at work in the form of conflict, pain, suffering, injustice and idolatry, one whose mission is to demean and to destroy life.

People have changed

One of the most profound changes in the last century is the degree to which ordinary people changed terms of their self-understanding. Ordinary people today are more involved, less ignorant concerning how their world works, more demanding of their social institutions and less easily controlled by the powerful. This change in people's self-understanding combines with the technology and communications revolution in a way that sharply increases the power of ordinary people. The value of local participation and ownership in ministry derives its success from this profound change in people's self-understanding.

In Europe and North America, there is a clear shift in values from an earlier focus on economic growth and material success in favor of values focusing on maximizing well-being, such as more say in government, protection of free speech, more say in jobs and greater demands for beautiful cities and countryside, a more humane society and inclusiveness. It is deeply ironic that this shift in values has been accompanied by decreasing Christian commitment or a shallow gospel heavily captive to culture.

Global economy, technology and communications

Global communications, the technology revolution and success of free markets across the world have created a driving force called globalization. The world is open for business 24 hours a day and information is available virtually anywhere at any time.

Transnational corporations promote, and often create, economic integration as they make investment decisions, move their money among multiple currencies, minimize their risk and make money by taking advantage of the gaps and inconsistencies between national markets. The internationalization of capital markets means countries are losing control of their currencies, commodity pricing and capital markets. Being large, international and technologically advanced is a competitive advantage in this kind of world. Being small, poor or technologically underdeveloped leaves you outside the field of play.

The global reach of communications and the power of the technology revolution mean that the media and advertising are able to become more local and personal. Magazines arrive with your address printed on the cover, or even arrive custom made to your e-mail address. The Internet allows highly personalized donor relations management, often to the point of raising concerns for privacy. Access to the Internet means news, knowledge, and sadly, pornography.

Using technology to manipulate information and to innovate is the engine of the new global economy. Those who have the skill, education and intelligence to create value with information will be the core workers of tomorrow.

Governance has also become globalized. The United Nations struggles to function as the focal point of the "international community." Democracy is assumed to be a universal good. Human rights are becoming normative. Humanitarian intervention supersedes national sovereignty.

The power of identity and the need for meaning

Everyone needs an identity that is rooted locally. No one feels at home in a global world. Global communications,

technology and economic integration draw things toward a center, integrating them into a global matrix. Identity, in the form of ethnicity or religion, is a counteracting force, working to disperse power, making things more personal and local. As the poor find themselves with no place in the global economy, the attractiveness of their ethnic and religious identity will increase. This leads to a fundamentalism expressed in ethnic and religious violence and social turbulence.

Throughout the world, there is a resurgence of interest in spiritual matters. The hunger for meaning in the human heart remains unmet by economics or technology. The world no longer believes blindly in the self-sufficiency of science or human reason nor in the inevitability of human progress. Cyberspace is not human space and virtual reality does not provide a substitute for the purpose and identity that people need. People are searching for spirituality, although in this post-modern world, any spirituality will do. Religious pluralism is increasingly normative.

Vision of a better future

A vision of a better future drives people and institutions. For the international community, the preferred human future is peaceful, materially prosperous and democratic. Such a vision supports peacekeeping and eradication of material poverty through globalization. This is the dominant agenda of most Western governments, the UN system, the World Bank, the International Monetary Fund and the World Trade Organization.

The market system promotes the belief that the better human future is a product of self-interest and limited greed. The market tolerates poverty in that poverty is acceptable as long as it does not affect me.

Sadly, the Christian community seems unable to proclaim a compelling vision of the best human future as being one in which human beings love God and their neighbor.

Changing demographics.

The world's population growth rate is decreasing, yet the total population is growing in many countries in the South. The North is experiencing close to zero population growth and is struggling to find social policies that make sense in face of aging populations. The single larg-est human migration in the 20th century has been the one from the countryside to the cities—47 percent of the world's population is now urban and this growth is primarily in Third World cities.

While the West, China and Japan are graying, much of the rest of the world is young. One-third of the world's popu-lation is under the age of 15, and 85 percent of these young people live in the Third World. These children need an education, a place in society and a way to become productive. Without this, these young people will be a powerful force for violence and social unrest.

A new generation or cohort group of teens and young people in their early twenties has emerged and, for the first time in history, it is global. These young people are connected by MTV, the Inter-net and a global youth culture. There are 2 billion young people in this population cohort. Several scenario-planning groups argue that the global young person is a new driving force in the making.

We've just looked at six drivers that are shaping God's world. Five of them are largely human inventions and, thus, flawed and distorted by sin. Then there is the Holy Spirit of God, who nonetheless faithfully and unchangingly moves human history toward its ultimate culmination. Our mission call is to join God's Spirit and give ourselves to the emergence of God's kingdom in a world that seems unwelcoming and bent on going its own way.

Let's take a look at this world.

The Historical Context of Mission

Changing paradigms of mission thinking

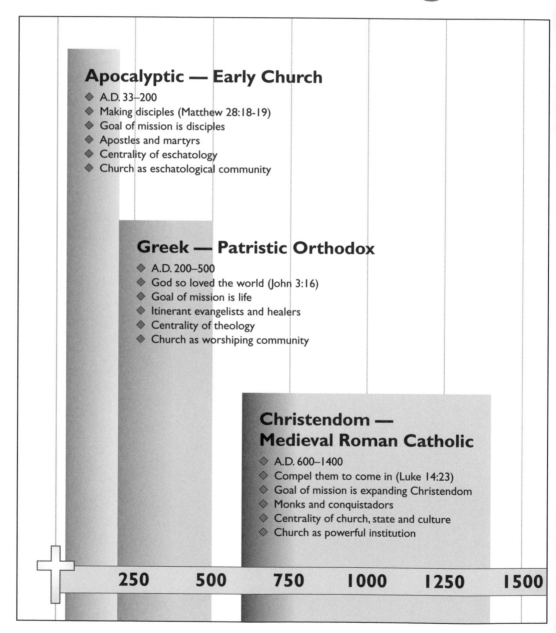

Apocalyptic — Early Church

◆ A.D. 33–200
◆ Making disciples (Matthew 28:18-19)
◆ Goal of mission is disciples
◆ Apostles and martyrs
◆ Centrality of eschatology
◆ Church as eschatological community

Greek — Patristic Orthodox

◆ A.D. 200–500
◆ God so loved the world (John 3:16)
◆ Goal of mission is life
◆ Itinerant evangelists and healers
◆ Centrality of theology
◆ Church as worshiping community

Christendom — Medieval Roman Catholic

◆ A.D. 600–1400
◆ Compel them to come in (Luke 14:23)
◆ Goal of mission is expanding Christendom
◆ Monks and conquistadors
◆ Centrality of church, state and culture
◆ Church as powerful institution

| 250 | 500 | 750 | 1000 | 1250 | 1500 |

Source: Adapted from *Transforming Mission*, 1991

Reformation — Protestant

◇ A.D. 1500–1750
◇ The gospel is the power of salvation for everyone who believes (Romans 1:16)
◇ Goal of mission is renewal
◇ Holy Spirit and reformed church
◇ Centrality of Scripture
◇ Church as reforming community

Modern Mission Era

◇ A.D. 1750–1950
◇ Come over and help us (Acts 16:9)
◇ Goal is salvation / better life
◇ Volunteers, missionaries
◇ Centrality of mission task
◇ Church as civilizing (Westernizing) community

Emerging mission paradigm for the third millenium

◆ A.D. s1950– ?
◆ They preached, drove out demons and healed them (Mark 6:12–13)
◆ Goal of mission is to disciple the nations for spiritual and social transformation
◆ All of the people of God transforming all of life
◆ Centrality of holism—life, deed, word and sign
◆ Church as pilgrim community

1500   1750   2000

The unfolding of mission history

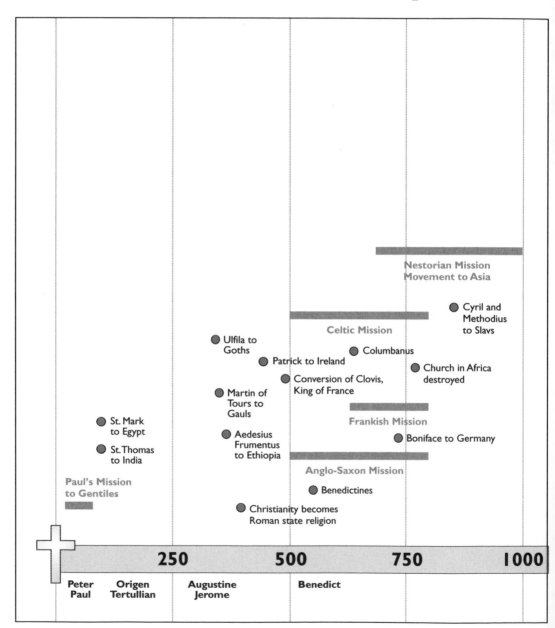

Nestorian Mission Movement to Asia

Cyril and Methodius to Slavs

Celtic Mission

Ulfila to Goths

Columbanus

Patrick to Ireland

Church in Africa destroyed

Conversion of Clovis, King of France

Martin of Tours to Gauls

St. Mark to Egypt

Frankish Mission

Aedesius Frumentus to Ethiopia

Boniface to Germany

St. Thomas to India

Anglo-Saxon Mission

Paul's Mission to Gentiles

Benedictines

Christianity becomes Roman state religion

250	500	750	1000

Peter Paul	Origen Tertullian	Augustine Jerome	Benedict

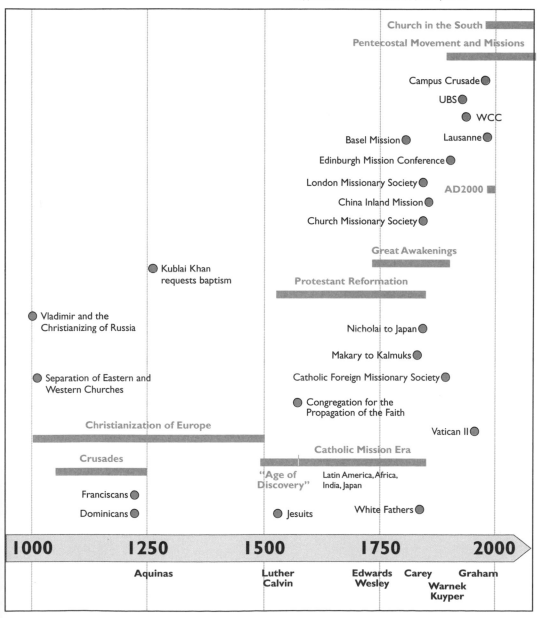

Sources: Developed from Neill, *A History of Christian Missions*, 1964
Lapple, *The Catholic Church: A Brief History*, 1982

Church in the South

Pentecostal Movement and Missions

Campus Crusade

UBS

WCC

Basel Mission | Lausanne

Edinburgh Mission Conference

London Missionary Society | AD2000

China Inland Mission

Church Missionary Society

Great Awakenings

Kublai Khan requests baptism

Protestant Reformation

Vladimir and the Christianizing of Russia

Nicholai to Japan

Makary to Kalmuks

Catholic Foreign Missionary Society

Separation of Eastern and Western Churches

Congregation for the Propagation of the Faith

Vatican II

Christianization of Europe

Catholic Mission Era

Crusades

"Age of Discovery" — Latin America, Africa, India, Japan

Franciscans

White Fathers

Dominicans | Jesuits

1000 — 1250 — 1500 — 1750 — 2000

Aquinas | Luther Calvin | Edwards Wesley | Carey Warnek Kuyper | Graham

The Christian church grows serially

The church in A.D. 100

The church in A.D. 400

The church in A.D. 1500

The church in A.D. 1990

Sources: Adapted from Andrew Walls, 1987
Operation World, 2001
World Christian Encyclopedia, 2001

◆ The Christian church began as a Jewish church and then moved to western Asia, becoming a largely Gentile church.

◆ By A.D. 600, the church spread to North Africa and to southern Europe. Its language was largely Greek. The center of gravity of the church lay between Rome and Constantinople.

◆ By A.D. 1000, the church had largely disappeared from North Africa and the Middle East in the face of a surging Islam. The center of gravity moved to Europe. Theology and mission became largely European.

◆ By the mid-20th century, the church was declining in the West. The center of gravity now lies in Asia, Africa and Latin America.

◆ At the beginning of the third millenium after Christ, the Christian church is now non-Western and its theology and mission are rapidly following suit.

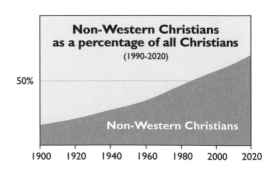

Non-Western Christians as a percentage of all Christians
(1990-2020)

50%

Non-Western Christians

1900 1920 1940 1960 1980 2000 2020

Christianity and Islam: The ebb and flow

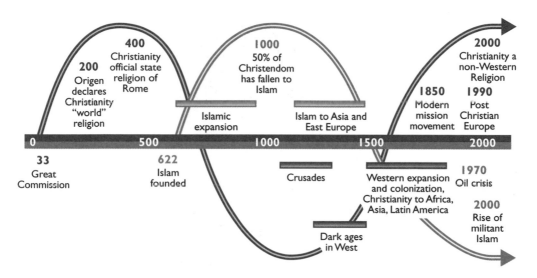

400 Christianity official state religion of Rome

200 Origen declares Christianity "world" religion

1000 50% of Christendom has fallen to Islam

Islamic expansion

Islam to Asia and East Europe

2000 Christianity a non-Western Religion

1850 Modern mission movement

1990 Post Christian Europe

0   **500**   **1000**   **1500**   **2000**

33 Great Commission

622 Islam founded

Crusades

Western expansion and colonization, Christianity to Africa, Asia, Latin America

1970 Oil crisis

2000 Rise of militant Islam

Dark ages in West

In the ebb and flow in God's history...

◆ By the time Islam arose in the seventh century, Christianity was a world religion and the official religion of the Roman Empire.

◆ Islam expanded serially from Arabia to North Africa and the Middle East, the Caucasus, North Africa, and Spain during the seventh century.

◆ The classical age of Islam (A.D. 775-1300) roughly corresponded with the Dark Ages in Europe and was the time that Islam extended its reach to Asia.

◆ During the nineteenth century and first half of the twentieth century, "Christian Europe" exerted colonial rule over most Muslims.

◆ From Islam's introduction into Africa until the mid-1970s, there had always been more Muslims than Christians in Africa.

◆ By the mid-1980s, there were more Christians in the non-Western world than in the West.

State
of the
World

The world by religion

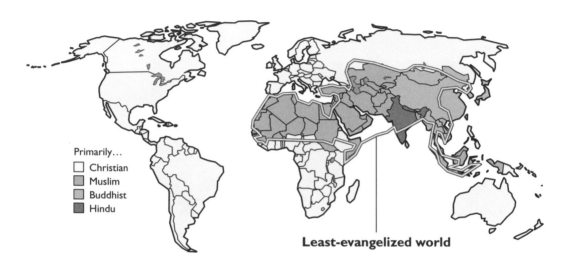

Primarily...
- ☐ Christian
- ☐ Muslim
- ☐ Buddhist
- ☐ Hindu

Least-evangelized world

In the 21st century...

- There are 2 billion people in the world who identify themselves as Christians.

- There are 1.2 billion Muslims. Muslims are the fastest growing major religious group, largely as a result of high birth rates.

- There are 784 million people who are Buddhists or who practice Chinese traditional religion.

- There are 811 million Hindus, largely in India.

- There are 918 million people who profess no faith at all.

Source: *World Christian Encyclopedia,* 2001

Growth in
world religions

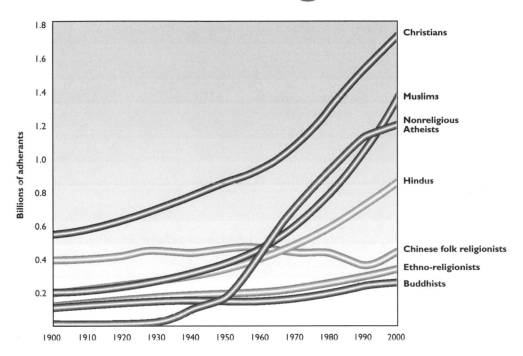

Impact of secularism

◆ The number of nonreligious grew from 3.2 million in 1900 to 918 million in 2000.

◆ This number of nonreligious began to decline after the fall of Communism.

◆ Being nonreligious or atheist is a largely 20th century phenomenon.

Staying power of folk religion

◆ Traditional or folk religion was the second fastest growing religious grouping after Islam in the last century.

◆ Traditional or folk religion failed to disappear in the face of modernity and the science and technology of the 20th century.

Sources: *World Christian Encyclopedia*, 2001
Operation World, 2001

The Muslim world

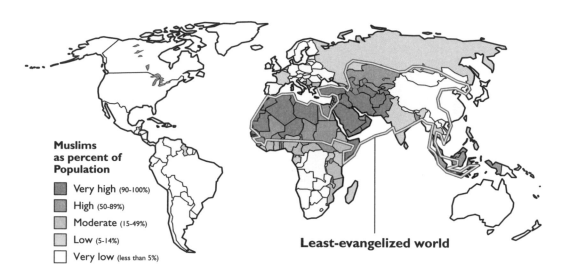

**Muslims
as percent of
Population**

- Very high (90-100%)
- High (50-89%)
- Moderate (15-49%)
- Low (5-14%)
- Very low (less than 5%)

Least-evangelized world

In God's world...

◆ Over 1.21 billion people in the world are Muslim.

◆ Islam is the fastest growing major religious group, largely as a result of population growth in Asia and Africa.

◆ The majority of Muslims live in South Asia and Africa.

◆ Over 80% of all Muslims have never heard the gospel yet regard Jesus as a key prophet.

Sources: *World Christian Encyclopedia*, 2001
Christianity Today, February 2002

Countries with Largest Muslim Population

Pakistan

India

Indonesia

Bangladesh

Turkey

Iran

Egypt

Nigeria

Algeria

Morocco

Source: *World Christian Trends*, 2001

Who has not heard?

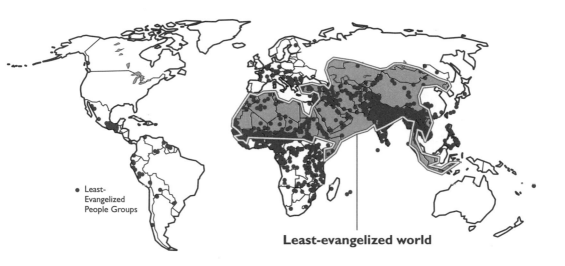

- Least-Evangelized People Groups

Least-evangelized world

In the least-evangelized part of God's world...

- ◆ Live **86%** of the world's people groups, of which less than 2% are Christian.

- ◆ Live over **80%** of the world's poorest people.

- ◆ There are **34** Muslim countries, **7** Buddhist nations, **3** Marxist nations and **2** Hindu countries.

Source: *World Christian Encyclopedia*, 2001

Countries with Largest Non-Christian Populations

China
India
Pakistan
Indonesia
Bangladesh
Iran
Japan
Turkey
Vietnam
Nigeria

Religious freedom

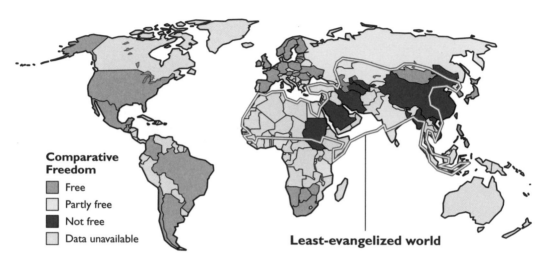

Comparative Freedom

- Free
- Partly free
- Not free
- Data unavailable

Least-evangelized world

Source: Freedom House 2001-02
(The Freedom Index is a measure of
political freedom and civil liberties.)

In God's world...

◆ In recent years there has been deterioration in religious freedom around the world.

◆ Religious freedom is highest in countries with Christian and Buddhist backgrounds.

◆ Islamic countries have the greatest restrictions on religious freedom.

◆ Over 70 million Christians were killed for their faith across 20 centuries. Over half died in the 20th century.

◆ The great majority of these martyrs have been Roman Catholic.

Source: Open Doors International, 2002
World Christian Encyclopedia, 2001

Worst
Persecution

Saudi Arabia

North Korea

Laos

Afghanistan

Turkmenistan

China

Vietnam

Bhutan

Iran

Pakistan

A world in conflict

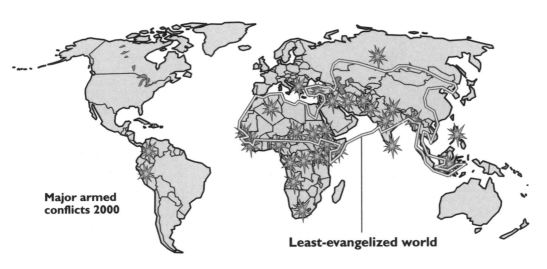

Major armed conflicts 2000

Least-evangelized world

Source: Project Ploughshares, 2001

In God's world...

◆ The number of major conflicts has risen dramatically from 10 in 1960 to 38 in 2000, affecting almost 21 million people.

◆ These 38 conflicts took place in 35 countries: 18 in Africa, 9 in Asia, 4 in the Middle East, 2 in Europe, and 2 in Latin America.

◆ Ninety percent of the casualties in today's armed conflicts are civilians.

◆ Africa accounts for 77% of deaths caused by conflict.

◆ Global military spending was US$740 billion in 1997.

Sources: *World Disasters Report,* 2001

State of the World's Children, 2000
Human Rights Watch World Report, 1999
Stockholm Int'l Peace Research Institute, 2001

Leading Arms Sellers 2000	*Leading Arms Buyers* 1996-2000
United States	Taiwan
Britain	Saudi Arabia
Russia	Turkey
France	South Korea
Germany	China

Source: *The Economist,* July 20, 2002

The world's poor

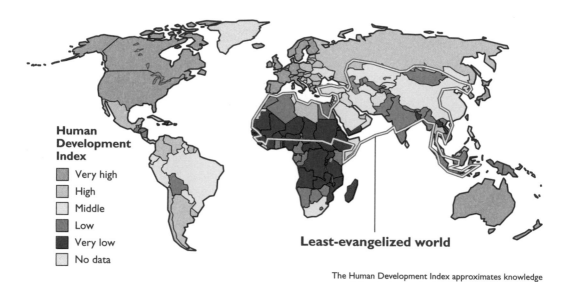

Human Development Index

- Very high
- High
- Middle
- Low
- Very low
- No data

Least-evangelized world

The Human Development Index approximates knowledge (education), a long healthy life (life expectancy) and a decent standard of living (real GDP).

In God's world...

◆ In the last 30 years, the developing world has improved as much as the industrial world did during the whole of the nineteenth century.

Countries with Lowest Human Development Index

Sierra Leone	Mozambique
Niger	Guinea-Bissau
Burundi	Chad
Burkina	Central African Republic
Ethiopia	Mali

◆ The number of people living on less than US$1 a day has fallen by 400 million since 1970, but was unchanged in the 1990s.

◆ Yet, still today one in five—1.2 billion people—do not have access to the basic social services of health care, education, safe drinking water and adequate nutrition.

◆ Women are 70% of the world's poor and two-thirds of the world's illiterates.

Sources: *Human Development Report,* 2001, 2002
State of the World's Children, 2001
The Economist, July 13, 2002

How are the children?

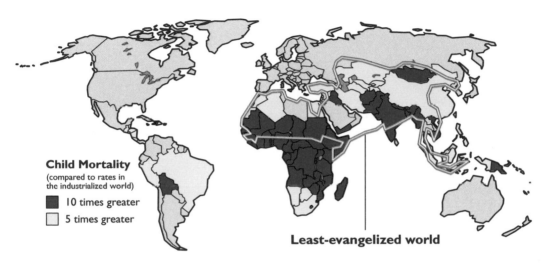

Child Mortality
(compared to rates in the industrialized world)

■ 10 times greater

□ 5 times greater

Least-evangelized world

In God's world...

◆ Child mortality, the average number of children per family, and primary school enrollment have all improved since 1960.

◆ Yet, 11 million children under five years die every year from preventable causes.

◆ Yet, over 250 million children will be working, instead of being in school.

◆ Yet, 5.8 million children fall prey to pedophiles and 625 million to child abuse.

Sources: *State of the World's Children,* 2001
World Christian Encyclopedia, 2001

Highest child mortality rates

Sierra Leone

Angola

Niger

Afghanistan

Liberia

Mali

Malawi

Somalia

Democratic Republic of the Congo

Mozambique

Source: *State of the World's Children,* 2001

Enough to eat?

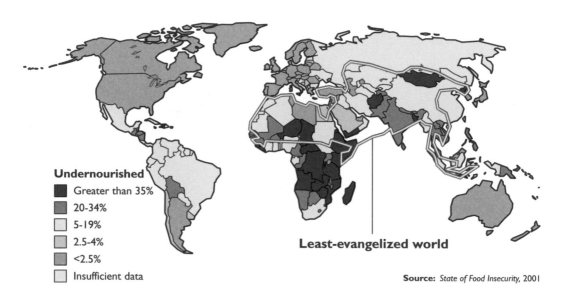

Undernourished

- Greater than 35%
- 20-34%
- 5-19%
- 2.5-4%
- <2.5%
- Insufficient data

Least-evangelized world

Source: *State of Food Insecurity, 2001*

In God's world...

◆ Each night 800 million people go to bed hungry, most of whom are women and children.

◆ In Africa, 34% of the population is under-nourished; in Asia, the figure is 16%.

◆ Civil strife and war are a major cause of hunger in the worst-off countries.

◆ There is enough food produced in the world to feed everyone.

◆ As many people are now malnourished in the West from eating too much of the wrong things as are undernourished in the Developing World.

Sources: *State of Food Insecurity, 2002*
Worldwatch State of the World, 2002
World Food Program Annual Report, 2002

Over Half of Population Is Undernourished

Somalia

Burundi

Democratic Republic of the Congo

Afghanistan

Eritrea

Haiti

Mozambique

Angola

Water scarcity

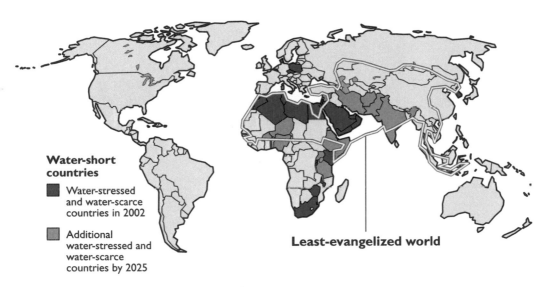

Water-short countries

◼ Water-stressed and water-scarce countries in 2002

◻ Additional water-stressed and water-scarce countries by 2025

Least-evangelized world

In God's world...

◆ Fifty-five countries with almost 1 billion people lack access to clean water and this situation will get worse.

◆ The United Nations is forecasting wars will be fought over access to water in the next 25 years.

◆ The world is not running out of water. The issue is one of quantity, location and access combined with a fixed amount of water and increasing population.

◆ Africa is most at risk as a result of population growth and the fact that 88% of the continent's water use is for agriculture.

Sources: www.itt.com/waterbook
www.bbc.co.uk, November 15, 1999
Independent (UK), March 5, 2003

Potential Water Hotspots

Jordan and Israel

Egypt, Sudan, Ethiopia

Turkey, Iraq, Syria

India, Bangladesh

Karnataka, Tamil Nadu

Libya, Algeria

Botswana, Namibia

Health divide

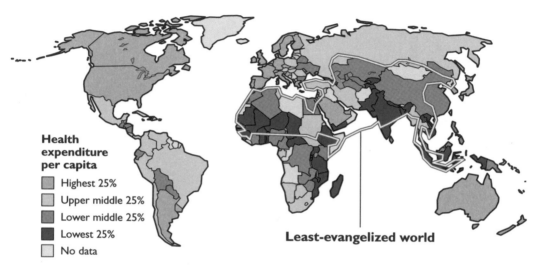

**Health
expenditure
per capita**

- Highest 25%
- Upper middle 25%
- Lower middle 25%
- Lowest 25%
- No data

Least-evangelized world

Source: *World Development Indicators,* 2001

In God's world...

◆ Infectious diseases kill more people every year than natural disasters.

◆ Tuberculosis, a disease of the poor once in decline, is now increasing again. Fifty million people have developed strains of tuberculosis that are resistant to existing drugs.

◆ Since 1945, 150 million people have died from HIV/AIDS, tuberculosis and malaria, mostly in the developing world.

◆ The developing world suffers from 90% of the disease burden yet has only 10% of the resources that go to health.

Sources: *The Economist Pocket World in Figures,* 2002
New York Times, June 29, 2002
World Health Organization, 1998

Least Access to Essential Drugs
Nigeria
Sudan
Angola
Burundi
Nepal
Moldovia
Cambodia
Gabon
Georgia
Haiti

Consuming the earth's resources

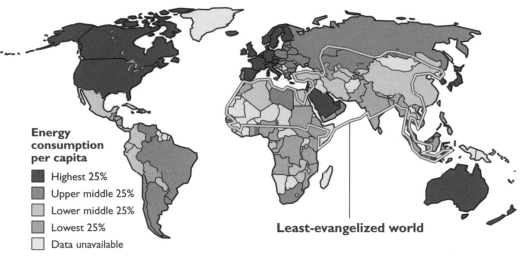

Energy consumption per capita

- ■ Highest 25%
- ■ Upper middle 25%
- □ Lower middle 25%
- ■ Lowest 25%
- □ Data unavailable

Least-evangelized world

Source: *Human Development Report,* 2001

In God's world...

◆ The greatest pressure on the environment comes from North America and Europe.

◆ High population growth adds people where the environment is already stretched to the limit.

◆ The least visible environmental trend is falling water tables, with the largest deficits in India and China.

◆ The amount of fresh water produced by the evaporation of rain is unchanged since 1950.

Sources: *The Economist Pocket World in Figures,* 2002
Worldwatch State of the World, 2000

Highest Producers of Energy (tons)	*Highest Consumers of Energy (tons)*
United States	United States
Russia	China
China	Russia
Saudi Arabia	Japan
Canada	Germany
United Kingdom	India
India	Canada
Iran	France
Mexico	United Kingdom
Venezuela	Italy

People without borders

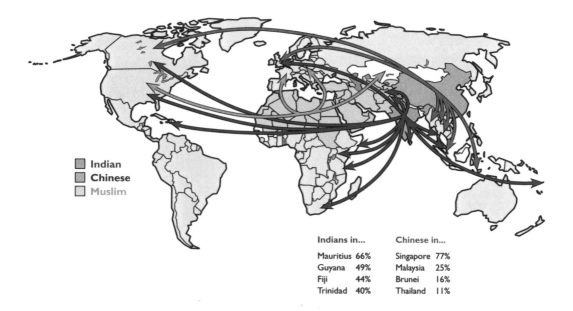

Indian
Chinese
Muslim

Indians in...		Chinese in...	
Mauritius	66%	Singapore	77%
Guyana	49%	Malaysia	25%
Fiji	44%	Brunei	16%
Trinidad	40%	Thailand	11%

The Chinese Diaspora

Indonesia	8.4 million
Thailand	6.4 million
Malaysia	5.6 million
Taiwan	4.4 million
Singapore	2.7 million
United States	1.9 million
Myanmar	1.6 million
Philippines	1.6 million
Vietnam	1.1 million

Source: *Operation World, 2001*

In these migrations...

◆ Over 55 million Chinese are living outside of mainland China.

◆ 22 million Indians are living outside India.

◆ Migrant workers remit US$75 billion to their home countries each year.

◆ The primary economic unit is the extended family.

◆ Today's Muslim missionaries are students, scholars, and refugees.

Sources: *Operation World, 2001*
The Economist, 1992
World Development Report, 1999

Following opportunity

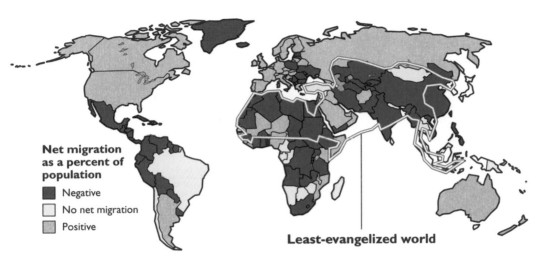

Net migration as a percent of population

- ■ Negative
- □ No net migration
- ▨ Positive

Least-evangelized world

Source: Project Ploughshares, 2001

In God's world...

◆ Over 150 million people live outside the country of their birth. About 13 million of these are refugees; the rest are mostly economic migrants.

◆ Migration is from the poorer south to the more prosperous north.

◆ Immigration is a major contributor to demographic change in many developed countries.

◆ Without immigration, Japan and western Europe will see declining populations as deaths begin outrunning births in the mid-2000s.

◆ Most international migrants come from developing countries, with China (14%) and Mexico (8%) as the largest sources.

Top Ten Migration Targets
1996-2000

United States	Rwanda
Germany	Liberia
Afghanistan	Hong Kong
Russia	Bosnia
Canada	Italy

Source: *Scientific American*, February 2002

The world by population

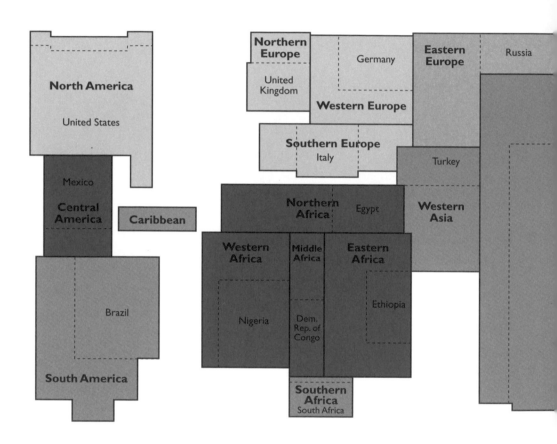

In God's world...

- The southern half of the world dwarfs the northern half.

- There are over 6 billion people and more on the way.

- The estimated doubling time for the poorest countries is 28 years.

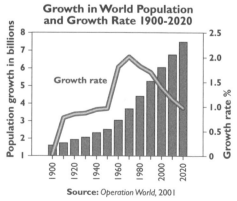

Growth in World Population and Growth Rate 1900-2020

Source: *Operation World*, 2001

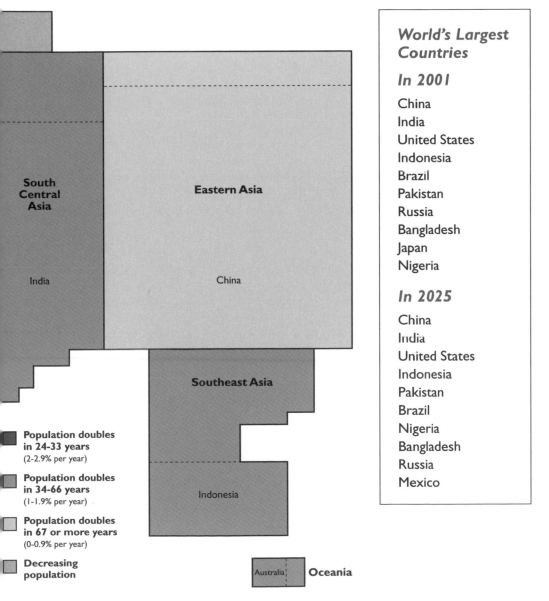

World's Largest Countries

In 2001

China
India
United States
Indonesia
Brazil
Pakistan
Russia
Bangladesh
Japan
Nigeria

In 2025

China
India
United States
Indonesia
Pakistan
Brazil
Nigeria
Bangladesh
Russia
Mexico

South
Central
Asia

India

Eastern Asia

China

Southeast Asia

Indonesia

**Population doubles
in 24-33 years**
(2-2.9% per year)

**Population doubles
in 34-66 years**
(1-1.9% per year)

**Population doubles
in 67 or more years**
(0-0.9% per year)

**Decreasing
population**

Australia | Oceania

Source: *World Population Data Sheet,* 2001

The world by income

Per Capita Gross National Income

(Purchasing power per person, 1999 data)

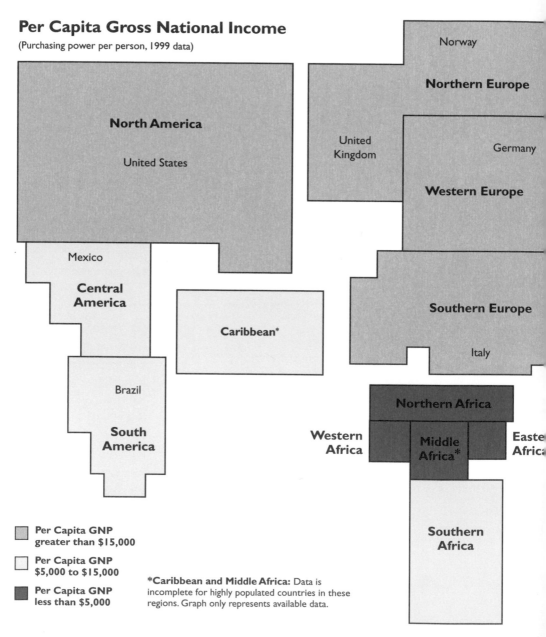

Norway

Northern Europe

North America

United States

United
Kingdom

Germany

Western Europe

Mexico

**Central
America**

Southern Europe

Caribbean*

Italy

Brazil

Northern Africa

**South
America**

**Western
Africa**

**Middle
Africa***

**Easte[rn]
Afric[a]**

**Southern
Africa**

☐ **Per Capita GNP**
greater than $15,000

☐ **Per Capita GNP**
$5,000 to $15,000

■ **Per Capita GNP**
less than $5,000

*Caribbean and Middle Africa: Data is
incomplete for highly populated countries in these
regions. Graph only represents available data.

In God's world...

◆ The northern part of the world dominates the southern part, with North America, Germany, and Japan accounting for almost 60% of the world's income.

◆ Almost half the world's families struggle with annual incomes of less than $4,700.

◆ Of the 925 million absolute poor in the world, 211 million (or 23%) are Christians.

Sources: *World Christian Encyclopedia,* 2001
State of the World Atlas, 1995
World Population Data Sheet, 2001

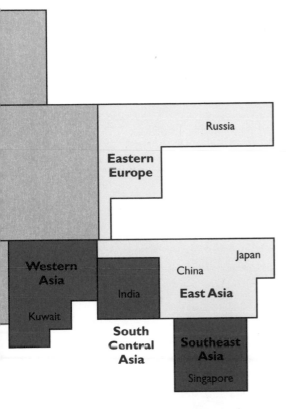

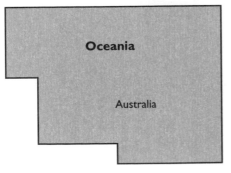

Source: *World Population Data Sheet,* 2001

Gross National Product	
(per person)	
Highest	**Lowest**
Luxembourg	Ethiopia
Bermuda	Burundi
Switzerland	Congo
Japan	Liberia
Norway	Myanmar
United States	Sierra Leone
Denmark	Eritrea
Iceland	Malawi
Sweden	Guinea-Bissau
Singapore	Niger

Source: *Pocket World in Figures,* 2002

The growing human family

Projected Population in 2025

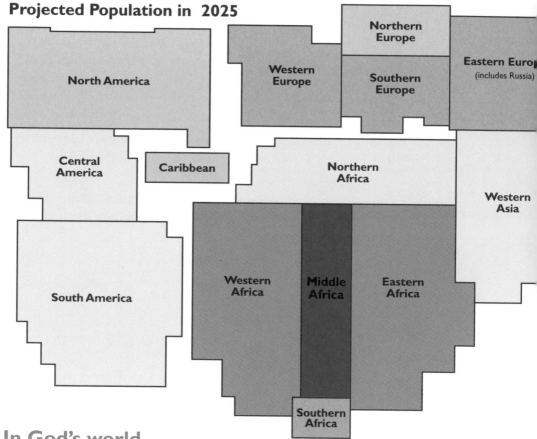

North America

Western Europe

Northern Europe

Southern Europe

Eastern Europe (includes Russia)

Central America

Caribbean

Northern Africa

Western Asia

South America

Western Africa

Middle Africa

Eastern Africa

Southern Africa

In God's world...

◆ During the 1990s, the world's population growth slowed considerably.

◆ Six of every ten people in the world will live in Asia in 2025.

◆ Only one of every seven will live in the West in 2025.

◆ Population in many European countries, Russia and Ukraine is declining as deaths outstrip births.

◆ Of the 83 million people born each year, 82 million are in the developing world.

Sources: *World Population Data Sheet,* 2001
World Development Indicators, 2002

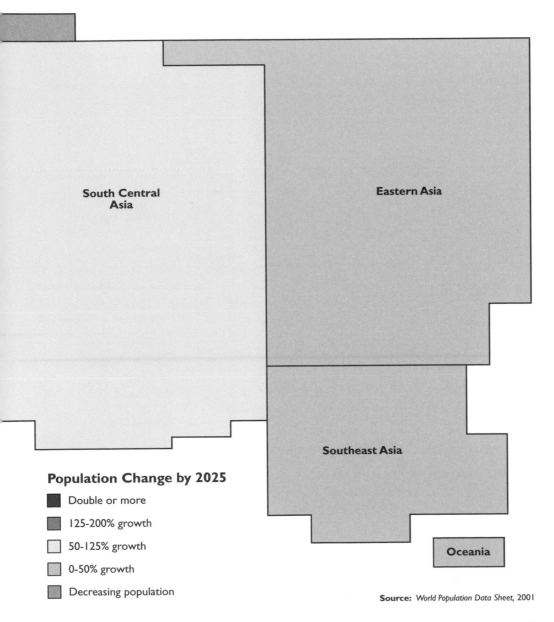

Population Change by 2025

- ■ Double or more
- ■ 125-200% growth
- □ 50-125% growth
- ■ 0-50% growth
- ■ Decreasing population

Source: *World Population Data Sheet*, 2001

South Central Asia

Eastern Asia

Southeast Asia

Oceania

Growing older, getting younger

Population by Age　　Developing Countries　Developed Countries

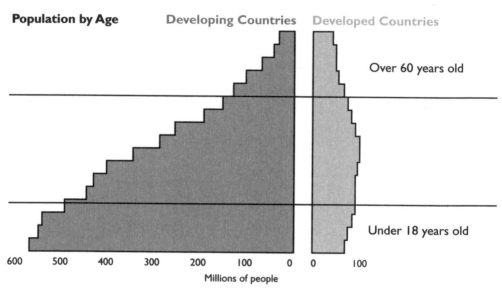

Over 60 years old

Under 18 years old

600　500　400　300　200　100　0　0　100

Millions of people

Source: *Kids Count Data Sheet,* 2002

In God's world...

◆ In Europe, over 20% of the population is over 65.

◆ Japan has more elderly people than children under 15.

◆ With negative population growth and increasing numbers of elderly, Europe and Japan face a welfare crisis.

◆ In Africa, half the population is under the age of 20.

◆ With positive population growth and large numbers of youth under 18, the developing world faces a crisis in education, nutrition and health care.

Sources: *Kids Count Data Sheet,* 2002
The Economist Pocket World in Figures, 2002
Far Eastern Economic Review, 1998

Highest Percentage Under 18 Years

Burkina Faso

Niger

Uganda

Yemen

Congo, DR

Angola

Somalia

Global economic integration

Global Communications

Technology Revolution

Success of Free Markets

GLOBAL ECONOMIC INTEGRATION

Fragmenting Forces

Rise in Fundamentalisms

Diminishing Sovereignty of Nation State

Movement of Peoples Refugees and Migrants

Integrating Forces

In God's world...

◆ The world is open for business 24 hours a day.

◆ Globalization of economies, global communication and the technology revolution mean that nation states are losing control of their currencies and capital markets.

◆ Global economic integration is uneven, leaving some people and nations outside.

◆ Twenty-four percent of the world lives on less than US$1 a day, down from 29% in 1990. Most of this good news was in East and South Asia.

◆ In the last 20 years, income inequality has risen in 66% of the countries of the world, particularly in Latin America, parts of Africa, China, and the West.

◆ The unofficial or informal economy, the world of barter and bribes, outside the protection of regulation and laws is estimated as one-quarter of the worlds' US$39 trillion GDP.

Sources: *Human Development Report*, 2001
The Economist, 28 August 1999
Cornia and Court, 2001

Global technology and communications

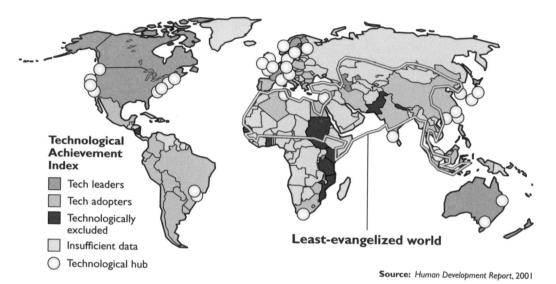

Technological Achievement Index

- ▦ Tech leaders
- ▢ Tech adopters
- ■ Technologically excluded
- ▢ Insufficient data
- ○ Technological hub

Least-evangelized world

Source: *Human Development Report,* 2001

In God's world...

◆ News and information is increasingly available all the time all around the world.

◆ A global youth culture—listening to the same music, seeing the same images and wearing the same shoes —is emerging, mediated by Music Television (MTV).

◆ As manipulating information becomes the engine of the global economy, the nonliterate, technologically disconnected poor may find themselves on the outside with no way in.

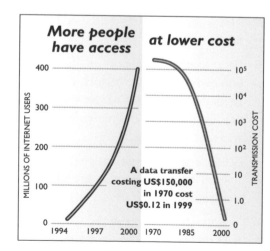

More people have access *at lower cost*

MILLIONS OF INTERNET USERS

TRANSMISSION COST

A data transfer costing US$150,000 in 1970 cost US$0.12 in 1999

Source: *Human Development Report,* 2001

Structures of sin

Annual estimated cost of "structures of sin"

Money Laundering	US$1.5 trillion
White-collar Crime	US$1.5 trillion
Financial Fraud	US$930 billion
Gambling	US$815 billion
Organized Crime	US$750 billion
Tax Cheating	US$250 billion
Drug Traffic	US$200 billion
Shoplifting	US$100 billion
Computer Crime	US$51 billion
Pornography	US$25 billion
Arms Black Market	US$5.8 billion
Electronic Warfare	US$5.8 billion
Credit Card Fraud	US$1 billion

In God's world...

◆ Just over 32% of the gross world product is related to the "structures of sin."

◆ The estimated cost of the "structures of sin" every year is US$9.3 trillion.

◆ The great majority of the activities that constitute the "structures of sin" are done by the well-off.

◆ The cost of extending basic social services—primary education, clean water and safe sanitation, and health care and nutrition—to people currently in absolute poverty is estimated at US$580 billion annually.

Sources: *World Christian Encyclopedia,* 2001
World Christian Trends, 2001
Newsweek, October 8, 2001

Economic freedom

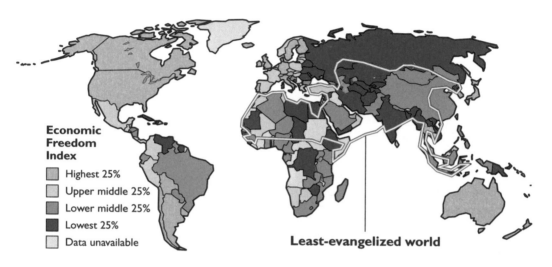

**Economic
Freedom
Index**

- Highest 25%
- Upper middle 25%
- Lower middle 25%
- Lowest 25%
- Data unavailable

Least-evangelized world

(The Index of Economic Freedom is a measure of money and
inflation, governments and regulations, takings and discriminatory
taxation, and restrictions on international exchange.)

In the last 20 years...

◆ No country with consistently high economic freedom has failed to achieve a high level of income.

◆ Countries whose economic freedom is in the lowest 20% experienced declining economic growth in the 1990s.

◆ There is a high correlation between economic freedom and high consumption.

Source: *World Audit of Economic Freedom, 2002*

Economic Freedom

Highest	Lowest
Hong Kong	North Korea
Singapore	Libya
Ireland	Iraq
New Zealand	Cuba
Luxembourg	Iran
United States	Laos
United Kingdom	Uzbekistan
Netherlands	Turkmenistan
Australia	Zimbabwe
Bahrain	Belarus

Having a say

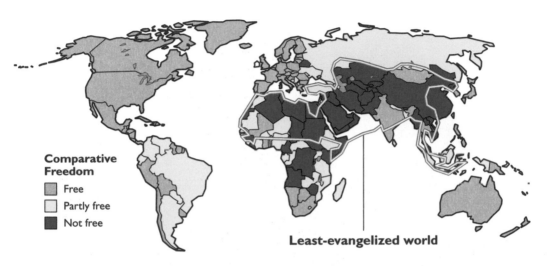

Comparative Freedom

- Free
- Partly free
- Not free

Least-evangelized world

Source: Marshall, 2001

In God's world...

◆ In the past 10 years, more than 100 developing countries ended military or one-party rule.

◆ Of the world's 192 countries, 121 practice some form of democracy. The 2.5 billion people in these countries enjoy 87% of the world's GDP.

◆ As many as 2.2 billion people living in 48 countries lack basic freedoms.

◆ While the countries with largest Muslim populations are electoral democracies, 28 of the countries rated "not free" have majority Muslim populations.

◆ Democracy and freedom are least well rooted in the Middle East.

Sources: *Human Development Report*, 2001
Freedom House, December 18, 2002

Least Free

Afghanistan	Libya
Myanmar	Saudi Arabia
Cuba	Sudan
Iraq	Syria
North Korea	Turkmenistan

The
Church
in the
World

Shape of the Christian world

Christians in 1900
(558 million)

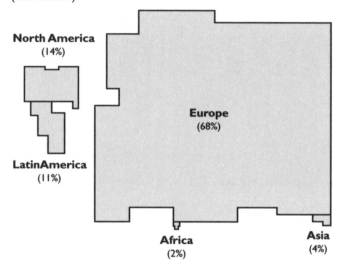

North America
(14%)

Europe
(68%)

LatinAmerica
(11%)

Africa
(2%)

Asia
(4%)

Christians in 2000
(2.0 billion)

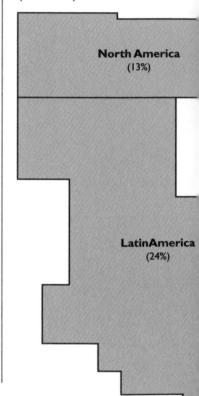

North America
(13%)

LatinAmerica
(24%)

In God's world...

◆ There has been a massive shift in the center of gravity of the church from north to south and from the West to East Asia.

◆ Over half of all Christians live in the developing world; nearly 70% of all evangelicals live in the non-Western world.

◆ The religious forms of the southern church are generally enthusiastic, spontaneous, fundamentalist, and supernaturalist.

◆ Two of every five professing Christians live in the world's poorest countries.

◆ The role of women is a pervasive element of the story of the growth of the church in the south.

Sources: *World Christian Encyclopedia*, 2001
Jenkins, *The Next Christendom*

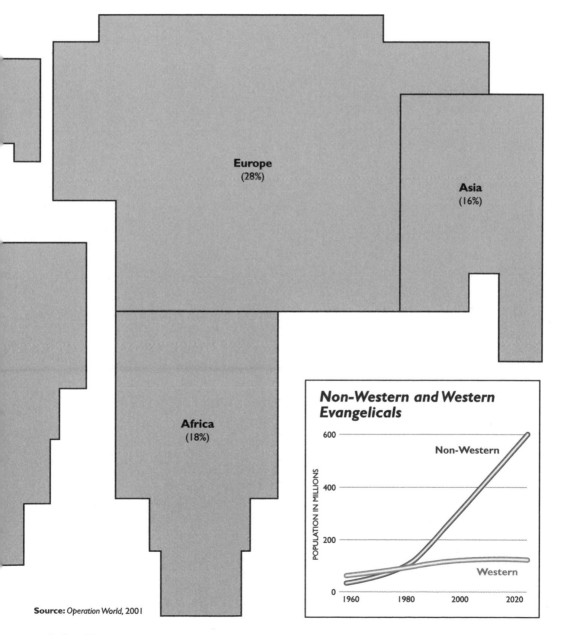

Europe
(28%)

Asia
(16%)

Africa
(18%)

Non-Western and Western Evangelicals

POPULATION IN MILLIONS

600

Non-Western

400

200

Western

0

1960   1980   2000   2020

Source: *Operation World,* 2001

State of the Christian church

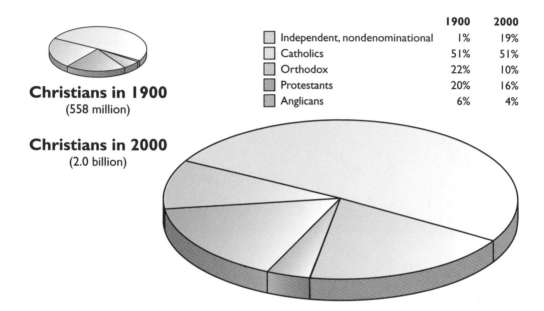

Christians in 1900
(558 million)

Christians in 2000
(2.0 billion)

	1900	2000
Independent, nondenominational	1%	19%
Catholics	51%	51%
Orthodox	22%	10%
Protestants	20%	16%
Anglicans	6%	4%

The body of Christ in the 21st century...

◆ Of those who self-identify as Christians, 640 million attend church regularly and work to obey Christ's gospel.

◆ The independent, nondenominational church increased ten-fold to 19% of all Christians today, mostly Pentecostal, charismatic in the Developing World.

◆ A little over 27% of all Christians are Pentecostals or charismatics. Pentecostals and charismatics increased 140-fold from 3.7 million in 1900 to 524 million in 2000.

◆ There has been increasing fragmentation as the number of denominations has almost doubled in 25 years to 34,000.

◆ One in seven, or 260 million, Christians live in absolute poverty.

◆ There are 1.2 billion nonliterate Christians who cannot read the Bible.

Source: *World Christian Encyclopedia,* 2001

Active Christians

Evangelicals by Region

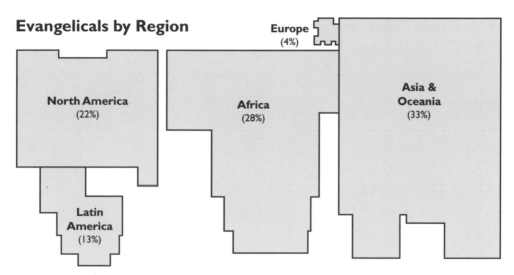

Europe (4%)

North America (22%)

Africa (28%)

Asia & Oceania (33%)

Latin America (13%)

Source: *Mission Frontiers*, December 2001
(Evangelicals are defined as "persons of evangelical
conviction who are active in spreading the gospel." These
numbers include Pentecostals and charismatics.)

In God's world...

♦ In a global village of committed Christians, there would be three Africans, three Asians, two Latin Americans, two North Americans, one European and a Pacific Islander.

♦ The evangelical movement is growing at 4.7% per year.

♦ Almost 40% of these people have no connection with a Western denomination or organization.

♦ People identifying themselves as Christians declined in Europe and North America during the 20th century, yet the percentage of committed Christians increased.

Flavors of Committed Christians

Conservative evangelical

Mainline evangelical

Conciliar evangelical

Anglican evangelical

Post-denominational evangelical

Catholic evangelical

Orthodox evangelical

Sources: *World Christian Encyclopedia,* 2001
Mission Frontiers, 2001

Signs and wonders

Pentecostal/Charismatic by Region

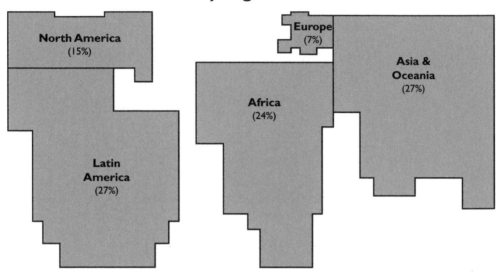

Source: *World Christian Trends*, 2001

In God's world...

◆ In 1900 there were less than 1 million Pentecostals/charismatics. Now there are over 524 million, about one-quarter of all Christians.

◆ Three-fourths of Pentecostal and charismatic Christians live in the developing world.

◆ Pentecostal/charismatics in 2000 are more urban than rural, more female than male, more under-18 than adults and more poor than affluent.

◆ Pentecostals and charismatics provide 38% of the global Christian workers.

Movements

Pentecostal	66 million
Charismatic	176 million
Third Wave *	295 million

* Independent and Post-Denominationalists

Source: *World Christian Trends*, 2001

The southern church of 2025

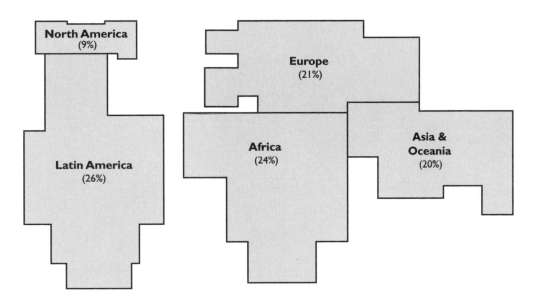

In God's world in 2025...

◆ Three-quarters of all Catholics will be found in Africa, Asia, and Latin America.

◆ The Pentecostal/charismatic movement will be over 800 million strong, located largely in the south.

◆ The southern churches are more conservative theologically than their counterparts in the north.

◆ The southern churches are deeply engaged in the supernatural expressions of the faith, including a Jesus of power who confronts and defeats the demonic.

◆ Across the south, church leaders are becoming national moral and even political leaders in a way no longer imaginable in the north.

Sources: Jenkins, *The Next Christendom*
Atlantic Monthly, October 2002

Largest Christian Populations in 2025

United States

Brazil

Mexico

Philippines

Nigeria

Congo, DR

Ethiopia

Russia

China

Germany

Source: Jenkins, *The Next Christendom*

The church in Africa

Christians and Muslims in Africa

- ■ Christian Majority
- □ Christian Minority
- ▦ Muslim Majority
- ■ Areas of Tension

In God's Africa...

◆ The Christian church first took root in North Africa in the second through fourth centuries.

◆ Before the mid-1970s there were more Muslims than Christians in Africa.

◆ Africa is experiencing the fastest church growth of any region.

◆ In Africa, the largest churches are Catholic, Anglican and Methodist.

◆ Responding effectively to the HIV/AIDS pandemic is the crucial test for the African church in the 21st century.

Sources: Walls, "Significance of Christianity in Africa"
State of Food Insecurity, 2002
Jenkins, The Next Christendom

The Largest Christian Majorities (among larger countries)	
Congo, DR	95%
Angola	94%
Burundi	90%
Uganda	89%
Zambia	85%
Swaziland	83%
Rwanda	81%
Namibia	80%
Kenya	79%
Gabon	78%

Source: Operation World, 2001

The church in Asia

**Active Christians
in Asia**

- Over 10%
- 5%-10%
- 2%-5%
- Under 2%

In God's Asia...

◆ The Christian church went to Asia in the second century from the Church of the East in Syria, and again to Asia in the 16th century from Spain and Portugal.

◆ Over 60% of Asia's 312 million Christians actively witness to their faith, the highest proportion of any region in the world.

◆ Asian Christians have faced the church's greatest persecutions. Religious discrimination directed toward Christians is once again on the rise.

◆ The largest Christian populations are found in China (90 million), the Philippines (67 million), India (67 million) and Indonesia (26 million).

The Largest Christian Majorities
(among larger countries)

South Korea	32%
Kazakhstan	25%
Indonesia	16%
Singapore	15%
Hong Kong	10%
Malaysia	9%
Myanmar	9%
Kirgystan	8%
Vietnam	8%
Sri Lanka	8%

Source: *Operation World,* 2002

Sources: Moffett, *The History of Christianity in Asia,* 1992
Operation World, 2001
World Christian Encyclopedia, 2001

The church in Europe

Active Christians in Europe

- ■ Over 40%
- ■ 25%-40%
- □ 10%-25%
- ▨ Under 10%

Source: *World Christian Encyclopedia,* 2001
(Active Christians hold evangelical beliefs and
are active in sharing the gospel.)

In God's Europe...

◆ The most religious countries in Europe are Ireland and Poland.

◆ The stagnation and decline of Christianity in Europe is one of the most startling features of the 20th century.

◆ By 2050, the Anglican Communion will have 150 million adherants and only a tiny minority will be white Europeans.

◆ The future face of Christianity in Europe is found in the rich faith of its immigrant populations.

Sources: *World Christian Encyclopedia,* 2001
Jenkins, *The Next Christendom*

Least Responsive Megapeoples

Swedes

Russians

Lithuanians

Poles

Georgians

Serbians

French

Irish

Czechs

Italians

Source: *World Christian Encyclopedia,* 2001

The church in Latin America

Active Christians in Latin America

- Over 20%
- 10%-20%
- 5%-10%
- Under 5%

In God's Latin America...

◆ The Christian church came 450 years ago from Spain and Portugal.

◆ The rapid rise of Pentecostal and charismatic churches among the poor and now the middle class is one of the startling missiological facts of the 20th century.

◆ The largest population of Protestants is in Brazil (33 million).

◆ The income share of the richest 20% is 10-20 times that of the poorest 20% in most countries.

Source: *Human Development Report, 2001*

Source: *World Christian Encyclopedia, 2001*

The status of the Great Commission

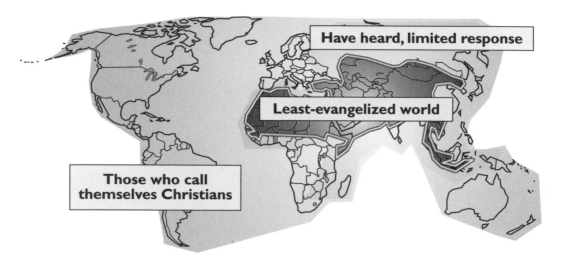

Have heard, limited response

Least-evangelized world

Those who call themselves Christians

In God's world...

◆ The percentage of Christians in the world has remained virtually unchanged at 33% since 1900. This has obscured an important sea change.

◆ Since 1900, the percentage of the world's people who have never heard the gospel has declined by 64% to 24%.

◆ Yet at the beginning of the 21st century, 1.6 billion people still have never heard the gospel.

Source: *World Christian Encyclopedia,* 2001

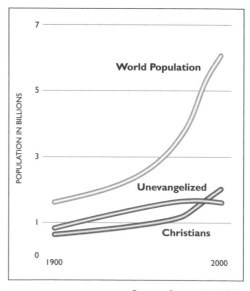

Source: *Operation World,* 2001

Sending and receiving

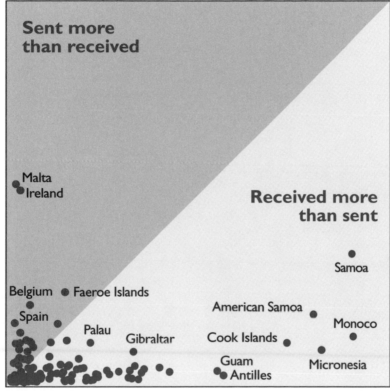

In the chart:

Sent more than received

Received more than sent

Missionaries sent ↑

Missionaries received →

Malta
Ireland

Samoa

Belgium ● Faeroe Islands

American Samoa

Monoco

Spain

Palau

Gibraltar

Cook Islands

Micronesia

Guam
Antilles

In God's world...

◆ Of the 141 countries where 60% or more of the people claim to be Christians, only 26 countries send more missionaries than they receive; 105 countries receive more missionaries than they send.

◆ The most oversupplied countries include New Zealand, many South Pacific island nations, Panama and Chile.

Source: *World Christian Trends*, 2001

Challenges to Mission

Who needs to hear?

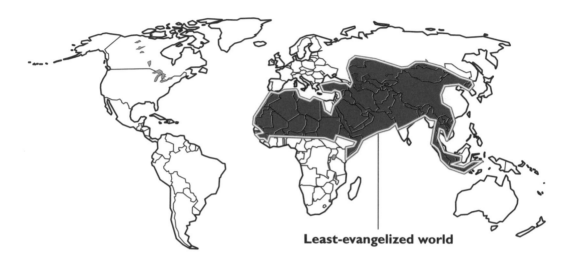

Least-evangelized world

In God's world...

◆ Over 1.6 billion people live in the least-evangelized world. Over 382 million live in a culture without a witnessing church.

◆ There are 2,000 people groups who have never heard the Good News.

◆ Only 0.3% of the global income of all Christians is being spent on mission in this part of the world.

Sources: *World Christian Trends, 2001*
Operation World, 2001

Largest Least Evangelized	
Western Punjabi (Pakistan)	67 million
Han-Jinyu (China)	47 million
Han-Hunanese (China)	44 million
Awadi (India)	37 million
Bhojpuri Bihari (India)	36 million
Maitili (India)	32 million
Han-kan (China)	25 million
Northern Uzbek (Uzbekistan)	19 million
Sindhi (Pakistan)	18 million
Braj Bhakha (India)	18 million

Children and youth

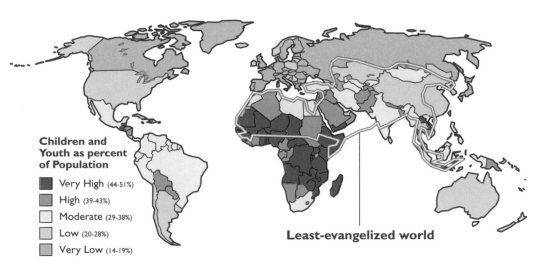

**Children and
Youth as percent
of Population**

■ Very High (44-51%)
■ High (39-43%)
□ Moderate (29-38%)
□ Low (20-28%)
■ Very Low (14-19%)

Least-evangelized world

In God's world...

◆ Thirty percent of the world's
population is under the age of 15,
and 90% of these children and youth
live in the developing world and
eastern Europe.

◆ The great majority of people make
life-shaping faith decisions before
they reach the age of 20.

◆ Seventy percent of the world's births
are to non-Christian homes.

Source: *World Christian Encyclopedia*, 2001

Most Children Under 15	*Highest Percentage Under 15*	
India	Uganda	51%
China	Niger	50%
Indonesia	Angola	48%
Pakistan	Benin	48%
USA	Burkina	48%
Nigeria	Burundi	48%
Bangladesh	Chad	48%
Mexico	Congo, DR	48%

Source: *World Population Data Sheet*, 2001

The greatest human emergency in history

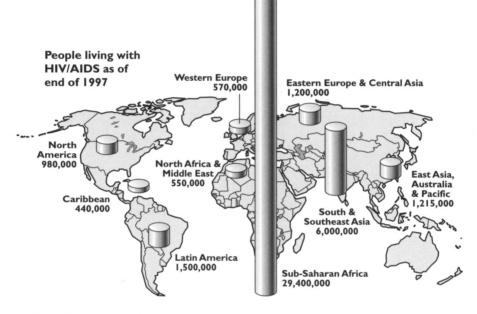

People living with HIV/AIDS as of end of 1997

Western Europe
570,000

Eastern Europe & Central Asia
1,200,000

North America
980,000

North Africa & Middle East
550,000

East Asia, Australia & Pacific
1,215,000

Caribbean
440,000

South & Southeast Asia
6,000,000

Latin America
1,500,000

Sub-Saharan Africa
29,400,000

In God's world...

◆ Over forty-two million people are living under the death threat of HIV/AIDS, and over 29 million of them live in Africa.

◆ AIDS has created 13 million orphans in Africa, and this could grow to 20 million by 2020.

◆ In Africa, the most prevalent victims are women and young girls.

◆ In Africa, AIDS is killing teachers faster than nations can train them.

◆ The next wave of HIV/AIDS will be in Nigeria, Russia, India and China, home of 40% of the world's population.

Sources: *UNAIDS Fact Sheet*, 2002
AIDS in the 21st Century
www.cia.gov

Highest HIV/AIDS Prevalence

Botswana	Zambia
Zimbabwe	South Africa
Swaziland	Malawi
Lesotho	Kenya
Namibia	Mozambique

The sinned-against

The sinned-against have no names or faces to most of us

In God's world...

- Over 1.2 billion people live on less than US$1 a day.

- Fifty-five countries with almost 1 billion people do not have access to safe water.

- One out of six human beings do not have access to any form of health care.

- There were 37 million refugees and internally displaced people in 2001.

- Over 2.2 billion people lack basic freedoms.

- Over 3 billion people are denied the freedom to teach ideas.

- Per capita overseas development assistance from 21 Western nations declined during the 1990s.

Sources: Gleick, *The World's Water*, 2001
The Economist, 8 January 2002
World Development Indicators, 2002
World Refugee Survey, 2002

Nomadic pastoralists

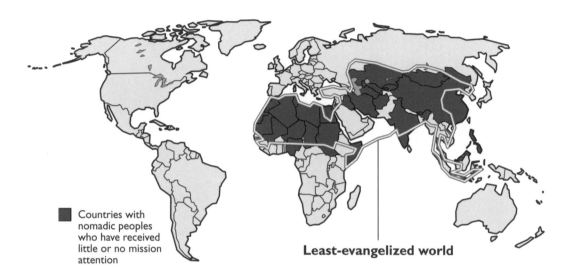

■ Countries with
nomadic peoples
who have received
little or no mission
attention

Least-evangelized world

In God's world...

◆ There are an estimated 20 million people living as nomadic pastoralists, moving from place to place with their herds.

◆ All but three of the 96 nomadic people groups are Muslim.

◆ Two-thirds of these nomadic people live in the northern half of Africa.

◆ To the nomadic pastoralists, the gospel is a demand to settle down, which means surrendering their culture.

Source: *Mission Frontiers,* December 2001

"When you can put your church on the back of a camel, then I will believe Christianity is for us."

— a Somali camel herder

Uprooted people

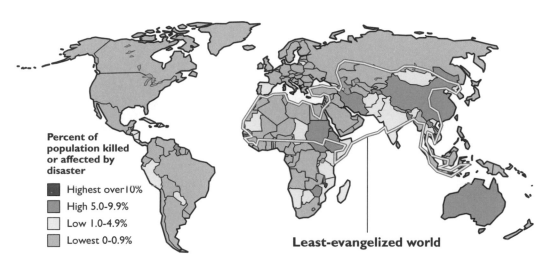

Percent of population killed or affected by disaster

- Highest over10%
- High 5.0-9.9%
- Low 1.0-4.9%
- Lowest 0-0.9%

Least-evangelized world

Source: *World Disasters Report,* 2001

In God's world...

◆ Half of the 37 million people displaced by conflict, persecution and poverty were children.

◆ An estimated 62% of the world's refugees in 2001 were Muslims.

◆ Over 227 million people experienced natural disasters or conflict in 2000; 83% of them live in Asia.

Sources: *State of the World's Refugees,* 2001
World Refugee Survey, 2002
World Disasters Report, 2001

Highest Number of Internally Displaced People

Sudan
Angola
Colombia
Congo, DR
Myanmar

Principal Sources of Refugees

Afghanistan
Palestinians
Myanmar
Angola
Sudan

Source: *World Refugee Survey,* 2002

The growing cities in the south

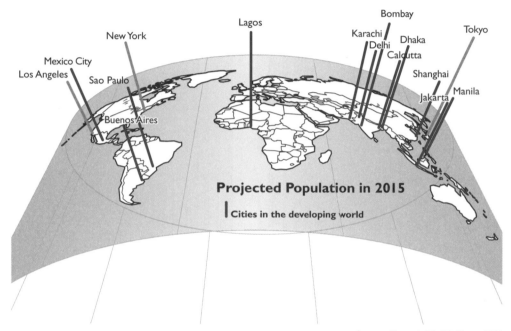

New York
Lagos
Bombay
Tokyo
Karachi
Delhi
Dhaka
Calcutta
Mexico City
Los Angeles
Sao Paulo
Shanghai
Buenos Aires
Jakarta
Manila

Projected Population in 2015

Cities in the developing world

Source: *Economist World in Figures,* 2002

In God's world...

◆ By 2025, more than one-quarter of the world's population will be poor and living in the squatter settlements of the developing world.

◆ Between 1960 and 1990, 60% of the growth of the cities was a result of births, while 40% was a result of migration from rural areas.

◆ Of all Christians, 62%—over 1.2 billion people—live in urban settings.

◆ There are more than 100 million street children in today's world-class cities—25% of whom both work and sleep in the streets.

◆ By 2015, there will be five megacities with populations greater than 20 million: Tokyo, Bombay, Lagos, Dhaka and Sao Paulo.

Sources: *World Christian Encyclopedia,* 2001
The Futurist, November/December 2001

Promoting equitable human development

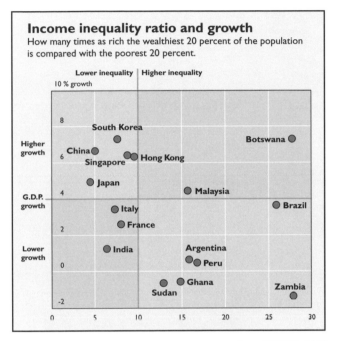

Income inequality ratio and growth

How many times as rich the wealthiest 20 percent of the population is compared with the poorest 20 percent.

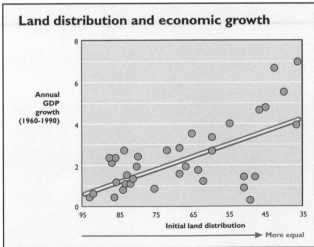

Land distribution and economic growth

Source: Deininger and Squire, 1997

Among God's people everywhere...

◆ More than three-fourths of the world's people live in developing countries. The richest 20% of the world enjoy 85% of the global income.

◆ The world's richest 1% receive as much income as the poorest 57%.

◆ Asia, Latin America, and the West have seen income inequality decrease since 1995.

◆ Africa and central and eastern Europe have seen income inequality increase since 1975.

◆ Recent economic studies suggest that greater income equality is compatible with faster growth.

Source: *Human Development Report, 2002*

Caring
for creation

High child mortality means more children
Low education of women means high fertility rates

Too many young mouths to feed
means no surplus capital

Too many children inheriting means landlessness

POVERTY

POPULATION

No potable water
Poor crop production

Lack of understanding of environmental issues
Inability to meet basic needs leads to overuse

Immigration to crowded urban slums
Increased use of pesticides and fertilizers
Increasing pressure on marginal lands

ENVIRONMENT

*Falling water tables, shrinking amounts of cropland
and leveling-off of ocean fish production
create challenges for feeding the world.*

Source: *State of the World*, 2002

The crucial importance of women

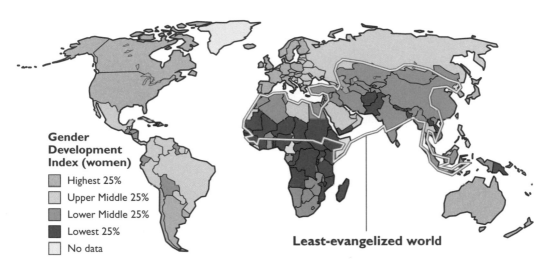

Gender Development Index (women)

- Highest 25%
- Upper Middle 25%
- Lower Middle 25%
- Lowest 25%
- No data

Least-evangelized world

In God's world...

◆ There is a very high correlation between female literacy and positive changes in under-five mortality, fertility rates, and economic development.

◆ Yet, the world average for female children reaching the fifth grade is only 63%.

◆ Yet, the proportion of women in all levels of schooling in the developing world is only 30%. In the West it is 81%.

Source: *Human Development Report,* 2001

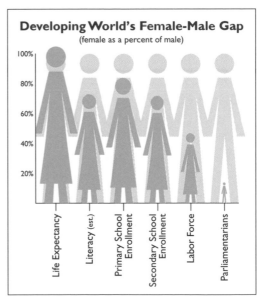

Developing World's Female-Male Gap
(female as a percent of male)

- Life Expectancy
- Literacy (est.)
- Primary School Enrollment
- Secondary School Enrollment
- Labor Force
- Parliamentarians

Sources: *Human Development Report,* 2001
State of the Future, 2002

Allocating our resources for mission

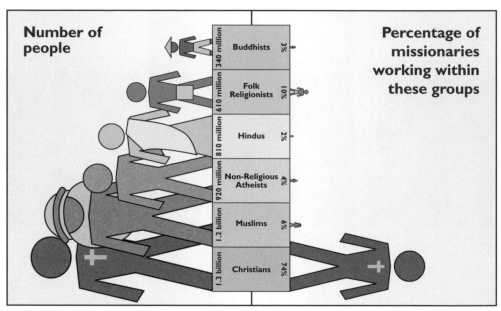

Number of people

340 million	Buddhists	3%
610 million	Folk Religionists	10%
810 million	Hindus	2%
920 million	Non-Religious Atheists	4%
1.2 billion	Muslims	6%
1.3 billion	Christians	74%

Percentage of missionaries working within these groups

Source: *The State of World Evangelization, 2002*

In the unevangelized part of God's world...

◆ About 5.6% of income to Christians went to foreign missions. Only 0.36% of this went to sharing the gospel with the 1.2 billion people in the least-evangelized world.

◆ Missionary sending from non-Western countries increased three-fold between 1990 and 2000.

◆ Only 0.4% of the Scripture distribution and only 3% of the languages for which the Bible has been translated are directed toward the least-evangelized world.

Sources: *World Christian Encyclopedia, 2002*
World Christian Trends, 2001
Mission Frontiers, December 2001

Protestant Missionaries Working in Another Culture

North America	71,088
Asia	69,203
Europe	22,897
Africa	12,442
Latin America	10,192
Pacific	9,452
Total	195,274

Source: *Operation World, 2001*

Conclusion

What's going on?

We've just looked at the world through a wide variety of windows: population, economics, politics, religion, children and church. Like a collage with many changing shapes and colors.

But these glimpses of the changing world of mission need to be summarized in a way that helps us get a feel of movement. Indicators of such movement are often called trends or trajectories of change.

I began this book with a list of driving forces in the world today. The six drivers I mentioned are like ocean tides, moving under the surface. Sometimes these drivers reinforce each other. Other times, they conflict, creating turbulence.

Tides, in turn, create waves that roll up on the shore. Waves are a little like trends or trajectories of change. They are what we see. They are what seem to affect us most directly. Global trends can be managed, even changed.

What follows here is one person's attempt to summarize the global trends affecting the lives of the poor and the lost in God's world.

Growing gap between the rich and the poor

Between 1980 and today, 15 countries enjoyed remarkable economic growth, and their 1.5 billion citizens have seen their situation improve. During the same period, more than 100 countries experienced economic declines, and their 1.6 billion people, almost half of whom are children and youth, have suffered through recessions, currency devaluations, crushing international debt and abuse by their own governments.

The world's poor often live in the unofficial shadow economy of street vendors, day workers and unregistered businesses. This informal economy is estimated at US$9 trillion. This shadow economy is the rawest expression of capitalism, existing on barter, bribes and illegal activities, devoid of the protections of regulation and law. Illicit drugs, street children, child labor, sexual exploitation of children and illegal small arms trade are normal and unchallenged in this shadow economy.

The invisible poor and the lost

Distressingly, the poor and the lost are often invisible to the Christian church. Within a band reaching across North Africa, including most of the Sahel, through the Middle East, and into the central Asian provinces, the northern part of the Indian subcontinent, Southeast Asia and western China, live 1.6 billion people who have little chance to hear the good news of Jesus Christ unless someone goes to tell them. Eighty-five percent of the world's poorest countries are located in this same part of the world. Yet only 1.2% of Christian mission giving is being invested there.

Increasing internal violence and conflict

In 2000, 38 major conflicts and wars occurred around the world. Over 540 million children are estimated to live in unstable or violent contexts. More than 2 million children died as a result of armed conflict in the 1990s and more than 6 million were seriously injured or permanently disabled.

Local warlords, unable to extract money from superpowers or governments, have turned to exporting local natural resources to pay for their armies while turning 300,000 children into soldiers. The long-term effects as these traumatized young men and women become adults creates a difficult future challenge. These local upheavals contribute to increasing numbers of internally displaced people and refugees.

Movement of people

Conflict, disasters and environmental collapse have dramatically increased the number of refugees from 2.5 million in 1975 to 15 million in 2001. To this one must add the 22 million internally displaced people who have migrated to another part of their own country to escape war and economic collapse. The great majority of refugees are women and children.

Toward three centers of economic power and the growing power of Asia

Asia, the European Union, and the United States will form the three global centers of economic power. In time, these shifts will call into question the current hegemony of the U.S. dollar, the World Bank and the IMF. India and China will become major players on the global stage. The so-called Christian West will have large Hindu and Buddhist cultures playing on an equal economic playing field.

Marginalization of Africa

Africa is being marginalized as the North shows signs of becoming disheartened with the seemingly intractable problems of uneven political leadership, wars, declining agricultural production and increasing population. The social impact of the HIV/AIDS pandemic is threatening to reverse 30 years of development progress.

At the same time, Africa is also the home of the world's fastest-growing Christian community. In the light of Liberia, Rwanda and Burundi, Africa's leaders are struggling openly with the question of the kind of Christians their churches are producing.

Polarization of power

Economic and political power is polarizing global and local institutions. Global institutions, such as the UN, World Bank, the IMF and transnational corporations, exercise global power, acting out their international roles in a global economy, playing god in the lives of the poor. Locally, power is held by local strongmen or warlords, manipulating local situations by force of arms paid for by providing gold, diamonds and oil to the global economy. Ethnicity and religion are shamelessly manipulated to create local power. The poor find themselves powerless in the face of these largely unaccountable centers of power.

Shifting patterns of governance

Not too long ago, governments were the primary and sometimes only source of governance, policy and accountability. This is changing. Governments are under increasing challenge for corruption and bad policy. Both their citizens and the international community no longer accept that governments can do as they like and take what they please.

While democracy seems to be a guarantee against major famine, it is less clear that democracy is the answer to poverty eradication that some thought. Countries in Africa, Asia and Latin America are discovering that there is more to a democratic society than just elections.

Some thought the United Nations would provide an alternative of global governance. In the case of Bosnia and Kosovo, the ideal of national sovereignty was set aside. In other situations, such as Rwanda, the United Nations could not marshal a response that might have blocked a genocide. The struggle between a multilateral approach to the world's intractable problems versus a state-led approach continues.

The changing shape of the Christian church

As mentioned in the Introduction, the center of gravity of the Christian church is now in the developing world, where more than 50% of today's Christians and 70% of today's evangelicals live. Increasingly, the church is more southern, supernaturalist, conservative in terms of social ethics and committed to missions. The southern church is holistic in its approach to living out the gospel. Word, deed and sign go easily together in a church that never separated the material from the spiritual as has happened for over a century in the northern church.

The emerging power and place of women

Those who study human development now know that women—their education, involvement and leadership—are unarguably linked to much of the good that social change seeks. Female literacy correlates highly with reduced child mortality, lower fertility rates, improved nutrition, better children's education and successful micro-enterprise development. Particularly among the poor, women do much of the work, produce most of the food and raise the children.

All of this creates an interesting irony when it comes to the girl child. Girls still receive less food, less health care and less education than do boys. Girls are still subject to harmful traditional practices. If women are the key to transformation, a greater emphasis on the care, nurture and development of girl children must become a priority.

The public health divide

The divide between the rich and the poor in terms of public health is very stark. Infectious diseases kill more people every year than natural disasters. Since 1945, it is estimated that 150 million people died from AIDS-related illnesses, tuberculosis and malaria, in contrast to the 23 million who died in wars over the same period. Children are especially vulnerable.

HIV/AIDS in Africa and Southeast Asia threatens millions of lives and the social well-being of whole nations. Unless a radical new medical option emerges, Africa will lose one-fifth of its adult population or more during this decade. The social impact is already catastrophic, as teachers, doctors and civil servants are dying. Too many African and Thai teenagers are heads of families. China, India, Russia and Nigeria are HIV/AIDS time bombs waiting to explode.

Market forces drive the decisions as to which new drugs are developed. Many research-based pharmaceutical companies have stopped investing in research of tropical diseases because of high costs and the prospects of limited financial returns.

Environmental limits

The world is experiencing limits in terms of what our environment will allow. The three parallel trends of falling water tables, shrinking cropland per person and leveling off of fish production from oceans combine as a serious threat to meeting the world's demand for food. Population growth is high in regions least able to provide for more people. Sub-Saharan Africa and South Asia will have 70 percent of the world's food-insecure people in 2010.

Poverty is leading to environmental degradation, which in turn creates more poverty. Environmental refugees, estimated by some to be as high as 25 million, are going to the cities and across borders.

Consumption patterns in the North make a far higher per capita impact on the environment than that of the rest of the world. A child born in the industrialized world adds more to consumption and pollution over his or her lifetime than 30-50 children born in the developing world.

Unless new and better ways of water management are developed, fresh water may emerge as the key limitation to global food production. The food supply of 500 million people today is being produced by an unsustainable use of water. The largest water deficits are in India and China, the two largest nations on earth. Some predict that the future major wars will be over access to water.

So what do we do?

In graphics and words, we have seen a world in pain. Many human beings are experiencing the world as one of painful toil. The world reflects the curse that accompanied the Fall: "Cursed is the ground because of you." The Creation is indeed "groaning as in the pains of child-birth." For far too many people, there is little good news.

So what do we do? How must we respond?

First, we must be sure we see what we are meant to see. Second, we are commanded to love God and our neigh-bor; our response begins from there. Finally, we are to look to Jesus and his compassion, compassion with an attitude.

Eyes that see truly

In Numbers 13 we find an interest-ing story. A team of Israelites was sent to explore the land of the Canaanites, the land promised to the newly liberated nation of Israel. Upon their return, they announced that the land did indeed flow with milk and honey, just as God had said. But, they also reported that the land is filled with powerful people and fortified cities. So overwhelming was their impression of what they had seen that they concluded, "We cannot attack

those people; they are stronger than we are. ... We seemed like grasshoppers in our own eyes ..." (Num. 13: 26-36, NIV).

Only Caleb disagreed. "We should go up and take possession of the land, for we certainly can do it" (Num. 14: 6-10, NIV).

The people of Israel listened to the others and rebelled against Caleb's vision and Moses' leadership. This failure to trust God and God's promise cost Israel 40 years in the wilderness while God waited for all who had been in Egypt to die before God gave the land to Joshua and a new Israel that had no memory of Egypt.

The reconnaissance team all saw the same things, the same fields, the same cities, the same Canaanites. Yet they returned giving these facts entirely dif-ferent meanings. Most saw power and threat in Canaan and inadequacy and weakness in themselves. Caleb saw a land promised by God and reacted with courage.

You have just finished reading, or per-haps thumbing, a whole series of graphics that describe God's world in many differ-ent ways. The key question is what does this mean?

Those of a pessimistic bent will see overwhelming poverty, pain and injustice, a dark world lacking hope. Some will see a world controlled by the prince of this world, working against life and life abun-dant. Both will be tempted to believe this kind of world is beyond the ability of the church to respond, too hard for Christians to do anything about. Or they will be tempted to seek only the saving of souls, leaving the poor and broken bodies, the unjust social systems, ignored.

The more optimistic will see a world of growth, opportunity and progress. Sure there is a lot that needs fixing, but things are basically getting better. The pain and suffering will be dismissed as ab-errations, holdovers from an earlier time. They believe the world, human reason and technological progress will eventually hold sway and all will be well. They will see the church as part of that progress and wish it to be relevant and modern. They will ask that the church stop being divisive, to stop saying that Jesus alone is Lord.

Caleb's view was different. Caleb saw the world as it was and that included an active and trustworthy God. Caleb did see the power and wealth of Canaan. He knew Israel alone was outmatched. But Caleb also believed God when God promised this land to a bunch of pow-erless slaves from Egypt.

Christians must insist on seeing the world as Caleb saw the land of Canaan, through the eyes of faith.

Christians need to see the world as it is—hard, inhospitable, and lost from God. Christians must see the church as it is— full of sinners, yet redeemed by the blood of the Lamb, God's only choice in response to such a world.

Christians need to believe God's promise: That in such a world and with such a church, the kingdom has come and will come in its fullness. That in God's time, there will be no more evil, no more pain, only life and life in all its fullness.

Christians need to believe, not in the failures that give evidence of evil, but in the small, tiny, often insignificant evidence of a kingdom that has come and is still coming. When we look at Mother Teresa caring for the homeless dying, at the food bank of our local church, at the ea-gerness of poor children now in school, we must recognize the kingdom plant that is growing from the tiniest of seeds.

Christians, like Caleb, must see what can be and what is promised, even when the temptation is to see otherwise. We must not let the world of pain, poverty, injustice and suffering drive us to inac-tion, to self-imposed retreat. Like Caleb, we must believe that we heard the truth when Jesus said that he came for life and for life abundantly, when he said that he would overcome this world.

We do not bring the kingdom; we can only believe in the king. We are commanded not to fix the world but to be obedient to what God demands of us.

Which world do you see?

Hearts that respond obediently

Jesus walked in the same kind of world in which we live today. Most people were poor and sick, and some were excluded from the community. The powerful took advantage of their own position. Rome was an oppressive empire. The religious folk were often more of a hindrance than a help. The demonic was busy working to diminish life and telling lies.

In this broken and suffering world, Jesus worked for life. He healed the sick, cast out the demons and preached the good news of the kingdom of God. Jesus prayed, acted and called together a community who were to be his body in this broken world after he ascended into heaven to intercede for us.

When asked what the bottom line was, Jesus' response was simple: Love God with everything you've got and love your neighbor as you love yourself.

This must be our response to the world described in this book. The pain, suffering and injustice, the hope and opportunity, all must lead us to seek God and to love our neighbor. We are to love all of them, their souls, their minds, their bodies and their communities.

The question of who our neighbor is has already been answered: Our neighbors are our own and those outside the gates, those on the other side of the world. God's good news is for Samaria and the ends of the earth, not just the good folks here in Judea.

Compassion with an attitude

It's popular these days to ask, What would Jesus do? The answer is to look at what Jesus did.

In the first chapter of Mark there is a very short story with a very big message. A leper calls out to Jesus, saying that Jesus can heal him of his leprosy if he wants to. "Filled with compassion, Jesus reached out his hand and touched the man." (Mark 1:41, NIV).

There are four things I want to say about compassion:

First, compassion begins with hearing or seeing.

The man called out to Jesus, and Jesus turned and listened to him. We need to look around us, to see those who are in pain, or are forgotten, or are on the sidelines. We need to hear their voices calling for help or moaning in pain. This book on God's world is intended to point us toward hearing and seeing.

Second, compassion requires that we go beyond seeing and hearing; we must be willing to feel.

The text says that Jesus felt compassion. The Greek word for compassion is derived from the word for spleen or intestine. This suggests that Jesus' stomach went into a knot when he saw the leper. The marring impact of leprosy on a human life wrenched his gut in a deeply visceral way. Jesus was always offended at the marred identity of the poor and the sick.

From where do such feelings come? We are relational beings, made in the image of a relational three-in-one God. When we are most keenly human, the well-being of others is closely related to our own well-being. This is why Jesus commanded us to love others as we love ourselves. Loving others is good for us. When we do not feel compassion for others, we are not fully human.

To be compassionate requires that we be truly human. We must be deeply moved with pity and outrage.

Third, while hearing, seeing and feeling is the launching pad for compassion, it is not compassion itself. Compassion is an action word when we see a world such as this book describes.

Driven by conviction and mercy, we must act and act since Jesus acted. He healed the man. The Samaritan crossed the road, setting aside his timetable, ignoring his ethnicity and risking his money. Gut-wrenching compassion makes us do things like this.

But there is more to this story. The action Jesus took was not simply ameliorative. Jesus did not simply relieve the leper's pain or bind his wounds and move on. After healing the man, Jesus instructed him to go to the temple for ritual cleansing, to be restored to his rightful place in the community of men and women.

Compassion is more than mercy, more than simple response. Biblical compassion has a bias in favor of restoration. Compassion is about helping people become who they were always meant to be: loved by God and neighbor, productive stewards in God's creation.

Compassion is hearing and seeing, feeling strongly and acting restoratively, doing all that God has given us the gifts to do.

Fourth and finally, biblical compassion carries an attitude.

"Filled with compassion, Jesus reached out his hand and touched the man." Jesus did not have to touch the leper to heal him. He could have simply spoken his word of healing and the leprosy would have left the man. Words alone would have been enough if healing had been enough.

What more is there? By touching the man, Jesus was adding a message to his compassionate act of healing.

We are well aware that a leper in first century Palestine was an outcast. Jewish law called for complete separation from the community. To touch a leper was to break the Law. Those in positions of religious and social authority were quite keen to see that this law was always upheld.

We also know that this preoccupation with the letter of the Law at the expense of what was good for human beings was an issue of considerable concern for Jesus. Jesus disliked seeing the Law applied in a way that harmed or limited people. Jesus went out of his way to expose this misapplication of the Law. Jesus taught that the Law is for relationships and human well-being. At the end of the day, the Law is about love.

In the leper, Jesus saw more than just a man whose body was marred by disease. He also saw a human being rejected by the community, cast out, made wholly other. The social identity of the leper also had been deeply marred. And Jesus knew that the religious and social establishment of the day believed this exclusion was both right and required by God.

Jesus knew that healing the leper was not enough. The deeper social issue had to be addressed as well. Jesus' decision to touch the man was meant to add a message to his act of compassion.

Touching the man was a radical critique of the dominant culture of his day, a critique that called into question the leaders of the people and their understanding of what God required. Jesus' act of compassion included the message that for the Christ, no one is outside God's kingdom unless they choose to exclude themselves.

In its fullest form, compassion is seeing, feeling and acting in a way that poses a radical critique of the dominant voices of the day, reminding them of what God, in fact, requires of them.

This short story in Mark carries the big message that the biblical Christian needs to do compassion in a way that creates a gospel commentary on the causes of human suffering. This means showing compassion to refugees, yet doing so in a way that unmasks the human greed and hunger for power that created the conflict from which refugees flee. Calling for biblical compassion to the one million internally displaced people in Angola needs to include exposing the malfeasance of the UN peacekeepers and naming the countries who are enriching themselves by helping the two sides of the war exchange diamonds and oil for guns.

Even when people are sick, there are often related social issues for which a message of gospel critique should be added to our response of medical care. Poverty is often as important a cause of poor health as are germs.

The bottom line is that compassion without a gospel comment concerning the causes of human suffering is not biblical compassion. Depending upon the underlying issue, the commentary can be personal, like the admonition to "Go and sin no more" to the woman caught in adultery, or be social like touching a leper whom everyone knows should not be touched. But the gospel critique is always there, beckoning us to turn around and truly enter the kingdom.

Of course, this idea of compassion with an attitude puts Christians, or church in mission, in a pickle. Compassion that critiques the powers that be can get you hurt. Unmasking the dominant culture is dangerous to your health. It can get you nailed to a cross. Helping without a message is safer.

But is it biblical?

Sources

"A Survey of the Defense Industry." *The Economist* (July 20, 2002).

"Armed Conflicts Report 2001." Project Ploughshares. www.ploughshares.com.

Barnett, Tony, and Alan Whiteside. *AIDS in the Twenty-first Century*. New York: Palgrave MacMillan, 2002.

Barrett, David, and Todd Johnson. *World Christian Trends*. Pasadena, Calif.: William Carey Library, 2001.

Barrett, David, George Kurian, and Todd Johnson. *World Christian Encyclopedia*. Oxford: Oxford University Press, 2001.

"Africa's Potential Water Wars." BBCi. (November 15, 1999) www.bbc.co.uk.

"Black Hole: The Shadow Economy." *The Economist* (August 28, 1999).

Bosch, David. *Transforming Mission: Paradigm Shifts in Theology of Mission*. Maryknoll, N.Y.: Orbis, 1991.

Brown, Lester, Christopher Flavin, and Hilary French. *State of the World 2002*. New York: Norton, 2000.

Brundtland, Gro Harlem. "WHO Stance on Health and Human Rights." World Health Organisation Press Release. Geneva (December 8, 1998).

Cornia, Giovanni, and Julius Court. "Inequality, Growth and Poverty in an Era of Liberalization and Globalization." Helsinki, Finland: UNU World Institute for Development Economics Research, 2001.

"Convergence Period." *The Economist* (July 13, 2002).

Deninger, Klaus, and Lynn Squire. "Economic Growth and Income Inequality: Re-examining the Links." Washington, D.C.: World Bank Finance and Development, March 1997.

Doyle, Rodger. "Assembling the Future." *Scientific American* (February 2002).

The Economist Pocket World Figures 2002. London: Profile Books, 2002.

Epstein, Paul. "Is Global Warming Harmful to Health?" *Scientific American* (August 2000).

Freedom House. "Freedom in the World 2002." www.freedomhouse.org.

Gleich, Peter. *The World's Water, 1998-1999*. Washington, D.C.: Island Press, 1998.

Glenn, Jerome, and Theodore Gordon. *2002 State of the Future*. Washington, D.C.: American Council for the UN University, 2002.

"Human Rights Watch World Report, 1999." www.hrw.org.

International Federation of Red Cross and Red Crescent Societies. *World Disasters Report 2001*. Geneva, 2001.

ITT Industries. *ITT Industries Guidebook to Global Water Issues*. www.itt.com.

Jenkins, Philip. *The Next Christendom: The Coming of Global Christianity*. Oxford: Oxford University Press, 2002.

———. "The Next Christianity." *Atlantic Monthly* (October 2002).

Johnstone, Patrick and Jason Mandryk. *Operation World - 21st Century Edition*. Bulstrode, U.K.: WEC International, 2001.

Kidron, Michael and Ronald Segal. *The State of the World Atlas*. London: Penguin, 1995.

Kids Count. "Kids Count Data Sheet."

www.kidscount.org (January 2002).

Landmine Monitor. (September 2001) www.icbl.org.

Lapple, Alfred. *The Catholic Church: A Brief History.* New York: Paulist Press, 1982.

Marshall, Paul. "The Current State of Religious Freedom." International Bulletin of Missionary Research. (April 2001).

"Measuring Up to Aid." *The Economist* (January 8, 2002).

"Megacities of the Future." *The Futurist* (November/December 2001).

Moffett, Samuel H. *The History of Christianity in Asia.* San Francisco: Harper San Francisco, 1992.

Myers, Bryant. "Global Context for Action." Monrovia, Calif.: World Vision International, 2001.

Neill, Stephen. *A History of Christian Missions.* New York: Penguin, 1964.

"The Next Wave of HIV/AIDS." www.cia.gov.

Open Doors International. *World Water List* (January 2002).

"Outpaced by Islam." *Christianity Today* (February 4, 2002).

Population Action International. "Water Short Countries in 2000 and 2025." www.populationaction.org.

Population Reference Bureau. *World Population Data Sheet.* www.prb.org.

"Red Cross Says Three Diseases Kill More Than Disasters," *The New York Times* (June 29, 2002).

SPRI Yearbook 2001. *Armaments, Disarmament and the International Security.* Oxford: Oxford University Press, 2001.

"State of Food Insecurity, 2001." www.fao.org.

"State of Food Insecurity, 2002." www.fao.org.

The State of World Evangelization. www.missionfrontiers.org.

"Storming the Fortress." *Newsweek* (October 8, 2001).

"Survey of the Defense Industry." *The Economist* (July 20, 2002).

Taylor, David. "Operation World 2001 - Reveals Emerging Global Trends." *Mission Frontiers* (December 2001).

UNAIDS. *2002 Fact Sheet.* www.unaids.org.

UNAIDS. *Barcelona 2002.* www.unaids.org.

UNHCR. *State of the World's Refugees 2000.* Oxford: Oxford University Press, 2000.

UNICEF. *State of the World's Children 2001.* New York: UNICEF, 2001.

UNOP. *Human Development Report 2001, 2002.* Oxford: Oxford University Press, 2002.

U.S. Committee for Refugees. *World Refugee Survey 2000.*

Walls, Andrew. "The Old Age of the Missionary Movement." *International Review of Mission* (January 1987).

"Water Scarcity could Affect Billions: Is This the Biggest Crisis of All?" *Independent/UK.* (March 5, 2003) www.independent.co.uk.

"Weight of History." *Far Eastern Economic Review.* (July 16, 1998).

"World Audit of Economic Freedom." www.worldaudit.org.

World Bank, *The East Asian Miracle: Economic Growth and Public Policy.* Washington, D.C.: World Bank, 1993.

World Bank, *World Development Report 1999.* Oxford: Oxford University Press, 1999.

World Bank, *World Development Indicators 2002.* Washington, D.C.: World Bank, 2002.

Reap a world of blessing

Resources to enable you to touch children and families around the world and be engaged with the poor.

Resources for education and mobilization

Youth and Family Opportunities

30 Hour Famine is an international movement to fight hunger and enable long-term changes in impoverished communities around the world. World Vision's 30 Hour Famine engages junior high, high school, and college students in a nationwide experiential hunger event. Participants fast for 30 hours—going without food to get a "taste" of hunger—while they learn about the causes of poverty and participate in community service projects. Funds raised are used to assist children and families in need both domestically and internationally. Approximately 15,000 U.S. churches participate annually in the Famine. Call 1.800.7FAMINE or visit www.30hourfamine.org.

One Life Revolution, a partnership between World Vision and Youth Specialties, mobilizes youth to make a difference in the lives of widows, orphans, and others suffering as a result of HIV/AIDS. Youth are encouraged to engage in this difficult issue through advocacy, education, and fund-raising. By raising money, youth can purchase life-sustaining items—such as a well or children's health care provisions—from the One Life Revolution catalog. Visit www.oneliferevolution.org for more information.

Love Loaf provides a tangible way for families to learn about ministering to the poor. This four-week educational and giving program includes family devotionals, bulletin inserts, and other materials that teach children and families about missions and how they can be part of God's work. Up to half the funds raised can be used for a church's mission projects. The remaining por-

tion is used in World Vision's international and ministry projects. Call 1.800.4LOAVES or visit online at www.worldvision.org/loveloaf.

The **Appalachia Summer Program** provides opportunities for church youth groups and families to engage in ministry with the people of Appalachia, home to some of our nation's worst poverty. In addition to service, the program focuses on leadership development, worship, and community building. To find out more about this short-term mission program and specific summer dates, call 1.800.877.5919 or visit www.worldvision.org/appalachiatrips.

World Vision provides **educational resources** through quarterly newsletters and catalogs of education and mission resources. To order, call 1.800.777.7752. Visit www.worldvisionresources.com to view available publications. We also publish an award-winning quarterly magazine that features articles on current issues, examines the causes of poverty and injustice, and profiles our work around the world. To order the magazine, call 1.888.852.4453.

Women's Ministry

Women of Vision provides educational, hands-on opportunities to engage women with people in need. Participants learn about world poverty through educational tools that equip them to advocate for the poor. Women of Vision has chapters in California, Colorado, Connecticut, Georgia, Illinois, New York, North Carolina, Oregon, Texas, and Washington state. To start or join a chapter in your area, call 1.877.968.4968, or visit www.womenofvision.org.

Global Involvement Opportunities

Sponsorship is now available for a child or an entire family. Through sponsorship you can build relationships that help children and families reach their God-given potential by tackling the root causes of poverty in their community. If you have a heart for children living in HIV-affected communities, ask about HopeChild Sponsorship—our newest sponsorship program that lets you reach out to children orphaned or made vulnerable by the AIDS epidemic.

Child: 1.888.511.6414 or www.worldvision.org
Family: 1.888.511.6493 or www.worldvision.org/family
HopeChild: 1.800.858.5853 or
www.worldvision.org/hope

***Gifts of Hope* Catalog** provides an exciting way to change the course of life for hurting children and families around the world while honoring friends and family. It includes more than 100 gifts, such as an ox and plow for poor farmers in Africa and clothing for a homeless child in the U.S. For a free catalog, or to order a gift to honor a loved one, call 1.888.511.6511, or visit www.worldvisiongifts.org.

Church Partnerships provide opportunities for U.S. churches to partner with specific communities around the world. These long-term relationships are designed to maximize a church's involvement and financial investment. Pastor's Vision Trips to Africa give church leaders a view of the AIDS pandemic and invite them

to join us in meeting the needs of children and families in communities that are especially hard-hit. For the latest schedule of Vision Trips, call 1.800.270.5629.

U.S. Involvement Opportunities

Every community has its own heroes—pastors, teachers, business owners, students, and parents. World Vision's U.S. Programs aims to empower and equip these local heroes to lead their communities along their own path to realizing their potential and

transforming their neighborhoods. Currently, World Vision is performing this vital work in Albany, Ga., Chicago, Los Angeles, Minneapolis-St. Paul, New York City, Seattle-Tacoma, Washington, D.C., and the Appalachia region. For more information on the following opportunities, call 1.800.393.7775, or visit www.worldvision.org/usprograms.

Vision Youth pairs struggling children and teens with trained mentors from their community. These

relationships help youth overcome difficulties and find hope for their future. As the heroes of tomorrow, youth discover their potential to revive their communities and their world.

Tools for Transformation equips local leaders and organizations with the skills to transform their communities. Local leaders learn key strategies to mobilize resources that serve local children, youth, and families.

The Storehouse provides resources such as clothing and shelter to revitalize neighborhoods and sustain families as they break out of poverty into a hope-filled future.

World Vision

34834 Weyerhaeuser Way South
P.O. Box 9716
Federal Way, WA 98063-9716
1.888.552.1508
www.worldvision.org

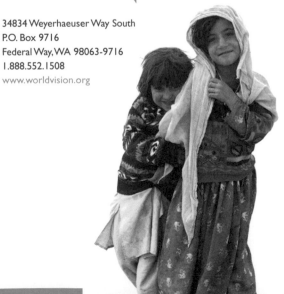

Other Publications from World Vision

DELIVER US FROM EVIL
An Uneasy Frontier in Christian Mission

A. Scott Moreau, Tokunboh Adeyemo, David G. Burnett, Bryant L. Myers and Hwa Yung, editors

368 pp.
2002
$34.95

Debating the nature of evil in the contact of God's sovereign love for creation, this innovative text explores key frontline dilemmas in understanding evil and its role in culture and theology of local settings.

ISBN: 1-887983-39-2

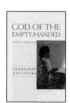

GOD OF THE EMPTY-HANDED
Poverty, Power and the Kingdom of God

Jayakumar Christian

224 pp.
1999
Y-003
$21.95

The author explores the relationship of poverty to powerlessness by masterfully integrating anthropology, sociology, politics and theology. Avoiding easy answers, he offers a new paradigm that can shape our responses to the poor and provide a workable framework for grassroots practitioners.

ISBN: 1-887983-13-9

LOCAL OWNERSHIP GLOBAL CHANGE
Will Civil Society Save the World?

Roland Hoksbergen and Lowell M. Ewert, Editors

363 pp.
2002
Y-025
$36.95

As global changes occur at breathtaking speed and our communities seemingly become more violent and desolate, many people have come to understand the importance of promoting human development in all corners of the world. Yet we must still grapple with the question of what role civil society should play in that effort and how it should go about addressing those challenges. This book covers the spectrum of that debate within Christian circles. The authors, approaching this topic from diverse disciplines and orientations, vary in their views and probe at the topic with great enthusiasm, exposing multifaceted insights, questions and practices of civil society, development and non-governmental organizations (NGOs).

GOD SO LOVES THE CITY
Seeking a Theology for Urban Mission

Jude Tiersma and Charles Van Engen, editors

315 pp.
1994
E-022
$21.95

The growing complexity of the world's cities demands a fresh look at the church's urban mission. In this volume an international team of urban practitioners explore the most urgent issues facing those who minister in today's cities. The team's unique methodology leads us toward a new theology of urban mission.

CHILDREN AFFECTED BY HIV/AIDS
Compassionate Care

Phyllis Kilbourn, editor

224 pp.
2002
K-013
$23.95

Phyllis Kilbourn and others tackle the very difficult issues surrounding the problems of children who are affected by the loss of parents or crucial caregivers due to AIDS. Kilbourn also recommends actions for caregivers when their faith and energy are tested by circumstance.

ISBN: 1-887983-28-7

World Vision

EMPOWERING THE POOR
**Community Organizing among
the city's rag, tag and bobtail'**
Robert C. Linthicum

Linthicum defines a new strategy that
goes beyond the superficial attempts
of the past to empower the poor
through faith-based community
organizing. These principles were
applied by World Vision in its work
in urban slums in 21 cities around
the world and resulted in 28 slum
community organizations, the
development of 52 businesses, and
the building of more than 2,000
homes.

118 pp.
1991
F-004
$9.95

CRY OF THE URBAN POOR
Viv Grigg

Grigg's follow-up to his best-selling
Companion to the Poor takes a closer
look at church planting principles for
developing a church that does not
treat people in isolation from their
surroundings. Church planters will find
this work a valuable resource.

295 pp.
1992
E-002
$11.95

CHILDREN IN CRISIS
Phyllis Kilbourn, editor

AIDS, abandonment, sexual abuse,
forced labor, war, urban violence and
girl-child discrimination destroy far
too many children's lives around the
world. Kilbourn moves you to a biblical
response to these global crises.

ISBN: 0-912552-97-2

304 pp.
1996
R-016
$21.95

STRESS AND TRAUMA HANDBOOK
**Strategies for Flourishing in
Demanding Environments**
John Fawcett, editor

How does stress impact human
functioning? What are the signs of
burn-out? What steps can be taken to
reduce the effect of stress and strain?
How does this research affect the
practicalities of everyday humanitarian
work?

The answer to these questions are
presented along with real stories, a
series of check lists, stress indicators
and burn-out monitors to track the
well-being of all workers. The focus is
on finding a way to grow and thrive in
these circumstances while continuing
to work, build strong relationships
and be proactive in life. The results
of this innovative research is sure to
benefit anyone who finds themselves
in demanding environments.

ISBN: 1-887983-52-X

272 pp.
2003
S-084
$29.95

GOD'S STEWARDS
**The Role of Christians in
Creation Care**
Don Brandt, editor

Forward by Eugene H. Peterson
Addressing the responsibility Christians
share in the practice of creation care,
this book examines the different
environmental heresies abounding
among Christians to provide a clearer
understanding of what it means to be
involved in sustainable development.
Written as a call to recognize our
role in faithful stewardship of God's
creation.

ISBN: 1-887983-42-2

112 pp
2002
F-034
$12.95